"In this important and highly informative book Susan Pacey draws on her research and extensive professional experience to bring together body, mind and relationship in addressing the untapped potential of psychosexual therapy. She provides a theoretically grounded basis for overcoming the dualism that has restricted its development for decades. *Sensate Focus and the Psyche* should be required reading for therapists of every persuasion who work with adult sexuality."

       – **Christopher Clulow PhD**, *Senior Fellow,*
Tavistock Institute of Medical Psychology

"In this extremely lucid book, Dr. Susan Pacey has provided us with a detailed exploration of the sensate focus approach to couple work with much wisdom, exploring the very close links to the more traditional, familiar forms of psychotherapy. By integrating these different bodies of theory and clinical insight, Pacey has succeeded in encouraging couple psychotherapists to speak about bodily sex in a more direct manner, while also inspiring sex therapists to think more psychoanalytically. Both students and senior practitioners alike will find this well-documented and thoughtful text of great inspiration."

       – **Professor Brett Kahr**, *Senior Fellow, Tavistock Institute of Medical*
Psychology, London; Visiting Professor, Psychoanalysis and Mental Health,
Regent's University London; author, Sex and the Psyche

"*Sensate Focus and the Psyche* advances previous efforts to integrate psychoanalytic concepts and sensate focus exercises to treat sexual problems. Numerous clinical vignettes add richness to the ideas and encourage clinicians to use sensate focus exercises in new and imaginative ways, thereby deepening the treatment."

       – **Norma J. Caruso, PsyD**, *Associate Clinical Professor,*
VCU School of Medicine; International Psychotherapy Institute, USA

Sensate Focus and the Psyche

Sensate Focus and the Psyche explores in depth both psychoanalytic and psychosexual perspectives of sensate focus, a programme of touching exercises for couples with sexual problems, and in so doing provides an original, integrated model for understanding the conscious and unconscious impact of this tactile intervention on couples in treatment.

Susan Pacey reviews the historical relationship between psychoanalysis and sex therapy and the splitting of mind, body and relationship since Freud. She illustrates how the tactile intervention can help repair the early life impingements on partners' individual development that mobilise anxieties about sexuality and shame in adulthood. Case studies illustrate how sensate focus can help conceptualise unconscious embodied memories, repair shame, encourage Winnicottian play, work through transitional phenomena and develop psychological space, establishing a platform for the healthy expression of adult sexuality. Pacey discusses how sexual desire and aggression are inextricably linked in the human psyche, proposing that sensate focus can help enable positive aggression necessary for sex and reduce the potential for partners' anxieties about their psychological separateness. Lastly, she proposes judicious use of this powerful, tactile intervention and highlights contraindications.

Sensate Focus and the Psyche will be essential reading for all psychotherapists who work with individuals, couples and families.

Susan Pacey is a psychosexual and couple psychotherapist in private practice in Central London and formerly in the NHS. She was awarded the degree of Doctor of Couple Psychotherapy by Tavistock Relationships and the University of East London in 2018. She is a teacher and author of several papers on sexuality and couples, and was an editor of the international journal *Sexual and Relationship Therapy* for seven years.

The Library of Couple and Family Psychoanalysis

Series Editors
Susanna Abse, Christopher Clulow,
Brett Kahr, and David Scharff

The library consolidates and extends the work of Tavistock Relationships, and offers the best of psychoanalytically informed writing on adult partnerships and couple psychotherapy.

For more information about this series, please visit: www.routledge.com/Routledge-Handbooks-in-Religion/book-series

Sensate Focus and the Psyche

Integrating Sense and Sexuality
in Couple Therapy

Susan Pacey

R Routledge
Taylor & Francis Group

LONDON AND NEW YORK

Designed cover image: The Distance (A Kiss With String Attached)
2003, Cornelia Parker. Photo: © Tate

First published 2024
by Routledge
4 Park Square, Milton Park, Abingdon, Oxon OX14 4RN

and by Routledge
605 Third Avenue, New York, NY 10158

Routledge is an imprint of the Taylor & Francis Group, an informa
business

British Library Cataloguing-in-Publication Data
A catalogue record for this book is available from the British Library

ISBN: 978-1-032-35739-3 (hbk)
ISBN: 978-0-367-36782-4 (pbk)
ISBN: 978-1-003-32829-2 (ebk)

DOI: 10.4324/9781003328292

Typeset in Times New Roman
by Apex CoVantage, LLC

Contents

Acknowledgements

Writing a new book about the use of sensate focus in couple psychotherapy has long been in my mind. It was, however, only on completion of my doctoral study in 2018 that my theories of this complex and controversial intervention, drawn from nearly 30 years of clinical experience, took proper shape, thanks to all the colleagues who became involved in my project in various ways.

For this reason I owe a great deal to, and wish to thank, all the participants in my study who gave so much of their time, professional experience and clinical wisdom in order to help me reach my goal.

Secondly, I wish to thank my commissioning editor, Christopher Clulow, for his continuous support and encouragement during the lengthy writing process, and for the inspirational teaching of couple psychotherapy theory and practice that I have received from him for the major part of my career as a psychotherapist. I owe much also to David Hewison and Avi Shmueli for their teaching of everything and sound guidance during the doctoral programme.

Thirdly, many thanks go Jane Seymour for her continuous interest in this project and for her experienced advice on sensate focus and her enthusiasm for the book. Jane is among my peers, close friends and family members whose support has been consistent and invaluable.

Fourthly I am especially grateful to Cornelia Parker for her permission to reproduce a photograph of her artistic work, *The Distance (A Kiss With String Attached)* (2003), on the front cover.

Finally, many thanks are due to Susannah Frearson, Saloni Singhania and their colleagues at Routledge for transforming my manuscript into a material book.

All case vignettes featured in this book have either been anonymised, and/or made composite and generalised, or permission to publish has been given by therapist and client.

Foreword

David Scharff

It is a delight to write this foreword for Susan Pacey's book that integrates sex therapy with psychodynamic thinking. I come to this task with the support of my co-editors in the Routledge Library of Couple and Family Psychoanalysis, because this is an area in which I also invested heavily early in my own writing. The fields of psychoanalysis, with its 130-year legacy, and sex therapy with now a sturdy 60-year legacy since its invention by Masters and Johnson in the 1960s, have each ignored efforts to bring together their areas of knowledge, experience and ways of working.

As soon as I began Susan Pacey's manuscript, I saw accumulating evidence that this book is a major contribution to sex therapy, a field that has continued to be practised but little psychoanalytically reconsidered. And at the same time, it enlarges the scope of psychoanalysis by providing avenues for understanding sexuality in a practical way. Pacey has applied developments in psychoanalytic theory and practice of the last 40 years to re-vision the potential for understanding the ways we can now deepen our understanding of behavioural sex therapy. This task, begun by the pioneer analyst Helen Singer Kaplan in the 1970s, and which my wife and I attempted to extend in following years, had been all but forgotten and neglected in the intervening years. The gap between the field of sex therapy and psychoanalysis that existed from the beginning has reasserted itself and in so doing, has continued to shortchange both fields.

In a funny way, this was less true near the beginning of the development of sex therapy as a new – and sometimes almost miraculous – invention. Masters and Johnson, following the innovations particularly of Virginia Johnson as the psychologist in their team, introduced many techniques and ideas about dealing with sexual anxiety and the way it was provoked and maintained by sexual misperceptions, lack of understanding and lack of knowledge. They taught couples to listen to and learn about their own sexual bodies, hopes, fantasies and fears, and to do so by using principally a psychosomatic language rather than a psychoanalytic one. In doing this, they confronted the fundamental flaw in psychoanalysis, which had been, up to that point, the only therapy that even attempted to address widespread sexual difficulties in couples and individuals.

There were at least two major shortcomings in the way classical psychoanalysis understood sex. First, Freud initially said that all development was about sex, gathering psychosexual development into his early concept of libido. In my reading of psychoanalytic history, by doing this, he coopted actual sex in order to make it stand for all of human growth, while simultaneously ignoring actual sex and its vicissitudes almost entirely. Now sexual fantasies and difficulties, as in the case histories of Dora, Little Hans and the Wolf Man, deployed sex too widely, as a kind of total explanation of developmental difficulty and of a wide swath of symptomatologies. In this way, although he always told the story of the families of his subjects, theoretically he ignored the attachment histories, the neglect and abuse in the families, and the transmission of parental difficulty and trauma to his patients. He discovered important things, but then, in his characteristic way, made too much of the very good things he had discovered. In this process, he came to ignore actual sex and sexual expression in the current life of his patients, an elision that much of psychoanalysis has maintained precisely because psychoanalysts in general (although with some obvious and outstanding exceptions) have continued to do.

Secondly, psychoanalysis, until recently, has insisted that the pure gold of analysis is the treasured relationship between the analyst and her patient. Indeed, they are often referred to as "the analytic couple". Their relationship is usually understood to encompass all we need to know about all other, real-life couples and family relationships.

Well, it just ain't so! For extremely good reasons, the "analytic couple" is forbidden to have sex. And while it is certainly permissible, even encouraged, to talk about sex, talking isn't doing! And thank goodness!

Furthermore (and again for good reasons), a patient's significant partners – husband, wife, same-sex partner, child, parent or friend – are basically treated analytically as figments of the analysand's inner world.

But they are far more than this. We know all too well that when we as analytic therapists invite a family, child or partner into the room with our patients, we almost always learn and see things in ways we could not have imagined, and which our patients have been unable – often unwilling, but more often simply unable – to tell us. And what we then see and hear makes an enormous difference.

Sex therapy brings these observations into the room. When the partners, who are now also our patients, tell us about what happened as they try to explore sexual life with each other, we can see and hear whole new realms, vistas that are opened by the direct way they tell us their experiences and observations, by their way of absorbing new information from their analytic sex therapist *and* from each other. Body learning and body exploration are extremely powerful, but so many patients and their purely analytic therapists have previously been shut off from that mode of experience, reporting and learning.

There is much more that Susan Pacey brings to her work, her understanding and to this book. She has, in a consistently scholarly and diligent way, drawn on the literature of advancing analytic ideas, and then drilled down to explain the detailed mechanisms of how her approach to using the sensate focus evokes a depth of feeling and a plethora of early developmental issues that come to populate the consulting room. She draws on recent analytic contributions, principally from British object relations and developments in understanding couples at Tavistock Relationships where she trained, invoking ideas from mainstream British analysts Donald Winnicott, Melanie Klein, Wilfred Bion, Peter Fonagy and Ron Britton, and also from thinkers at Tavistock Relationships such as James Fisher, Stan Ruszczynski, Chris Clulow and Mary Morgan. Pacey traces the history of the few authors who have attempted to cross the gap between sex therapy (and sex in general) and psychoanalysis. Then she shows us how invoking new understanding of the earliest mother-infant relationship, attachment theory, the role or absence of the father, and the role of trauma and neglect in early life can each shed light on blocks in sexual relating. She also explores how new understanding of the Oedipal development of triangular relationships can be helpful in the consulting room when the therapist inserts herself from her new vantage point, offering a third point of view that challenges partners' all-too-often locked-in views of each other.

To all this she adds an examination of the powerful role of the body and especially the sexual body in the privacy of self-experience and in intimate interaction, that is now – for the first time for such couples – available for description and examination.

Susan Pacey's thorough and original integration of psychoanalytic advances and behavioural therapeutic techniques, drawing on her understanding of the realms of clients' inner fantasies and equally from clients' live encounters, enriches her exploration as she expands our understanding of sex both in the outer worlds and in the inner worlds of her couples. As this book offers a major advance on our understanding, it issues a call that we embrace once more the detailed examination of sexual issues, behaviours and maladjustments so often at the forefront of difficulty for our individual and couple patients, and that we all continue to learn about these from a renewed integration of theory and practice, and from the patients themselves.

David E. Scharff, MD
Washington, DC
January, 2023

Chapter 1

Conceiving

Respecting an enduring intervention

This book is intended as a homage to sensate focus, probably the world's most famous, most used and yet most controversial psychotherapeutic-behavioural intervention in the treatment of couples with sexual problems. Designed as a phased programme of tactile exercises by Masters and Johnson (1970), sensate focus has been the cornerstone of psychosexual therapy (sex therapy) for over 50 years. This 'tool' has clearly stood the test of time, and for many good reasons, all of which are explored in the pages that follow.

Integrating approaches

My principal reason for writing a book on this topic is to offer psychotherapists an integrated way of thinking about sensate focus in clinical work, a way that takes into account body, mind and relationship. Such an approach is needed because in the past, therapies for couples with sexual problems have tended to be divided between the intra-psychic world of emotional-relational conflict (typically the province of psychoanalysis) and the conscious experience of behavioural and bodily response (areas that sex therapy has typically addressed). The essential flaw in attempts to separate mind and body in these two different therapies is that the psyche and soma are indivisible in human life. Both are always 'on', continually functioning at any time of day or night. How then did splitting come about?

The professional bifurcation between therapies can be traced back to Freud, who studied the underlying neuroses and psychopathology of sexual symptoms. His treatment therefore focussed on the mind. During Freud's life and until the late 1960s, remedies for patients' sexual distress were largely the domain of psychiatrists trained in psychoanalysis (Berry, 2014). A dramatic shift came in 1970 when William Masters and Virginia Johnson launched their own sex therapy, with sensate focus at the core of a residential, intensive, behavioural programme for couples. The celebrated duo deliberately excluded unconscious dynamics from their method, believing that phenomena such as countertransference could not possibly emerge in their institute's two-week course of treatment.

DOI: 10.4324/9781003328292-1

The bifurcation exemplified in Masters and Johnson's approach still lingers today and risks perpetuating an unsatisfactory service for clients. Practitioners working with couples' sexuality would ideally be integrated, that is trained and knowledgeable in both psychoanalytic and behavioural paradigms, confidently and comfortably moving between the two, if and when required in clinical work.

Understanding the power of sensate focus

There are further reasons for writing a new book on this topic. The first is that sensate focus is extraordinarily powerful and yet poorly understood. The profession needs to address this challenge. From my own experience and from that of my peers, using this intervention skilfully in couple psychotherapy takes years of practice (Pacey, 2018). Early in my career as a psychosexual and couple psychotherapist, I valued sensate focus highly, observing at times its remarkable, positive impact on partners' intimacy. However, I became equally aware of its therapeutic limitations and the range of anxieties it could provoke in clients: for example, the fear of suffocation and loss of self in sex. Such inner struggles are depicted in the image on this book's cover, a photograph of an original Rodin sculpture, The Kiss, adapted in 2003 by artist Cornelia Parker, who wrapped the famous lovers with a mile-long string, representing the claustro-agoraphobic dilemma of sexual relationships, as conceived by Henri Rey (1994).

Masters and Johnson's tactile intervention continues to be promoted as a cognitive-behavioural prescription in sex therapy training manuals worldwide and in many couple therapy textbooks and academic papers; for example, Giraldi and Graziottin (2007), Rosen (2007) and Weiner and Avery-Clark (2017). Nonetheless, its real value, as well as its constraints, has been underplayed, unexplained and under-theorised. The majority of publications describe the programme step by step, proposing that therapists teach partners sensual-sexual techniques and mindfulness, that is, how to focus on being in the moment when doing the exercises. Although couples' capacity to be mentally 'present' in the moment of intimate touch is critical to a positive sensual experience, the intervention requires a deeper level of understanding. In sex therapy texts, when clients report on their experience in the next session, therapists are encouraged to discuss partners' conscious thoughts, wishes, feelings, sensations, likes and dislikes (Weiner & Avery-Clark, 2017). These equate to an emphasis on the here and now, on physical and social factors affecting the couple. Generally speaking, psychological and relational phenomena are considered by only a few authors, for example Kaplan (1974, 1987), Scharff and Savege Scharff (1991), Green and Seymour (2009) and Caruso (2011). Few texts consider couples' particular *unconscious* processes mobilised by the therapist's introduction of the programme through to its conclusion. Understanding and working through these unconscious phenomena in the total transference situation, that is, in the three-way relationships between each partner and therapist and between partners, are critical to the therapeutic outcome of sensate focus in couple work. However, they receive too little attention in existing literature.

That said, over the decades thousands and thousands of couples have reaped benefit from sensate focus, which has the potential to play a role in the psychological development of partners, helping repair the past and encouraging new, healthier ways of relating. Anecdotal evidence is that without sensate focus, introduced sensitively and appropriately by the therapist, many couples of different ages and backgrounds would not have started or resumed sex (Scharff & Savege Scharff, 1991; Riley, 2007; Pacey, 2018). For these couples, their sexual relationship may be transformed and become a replenishing experience, giving partners a sense of connection with each other that was absent before treatment. Integrated practitioners are aware that talking therapy alone may not be enough to help couples improve unsatisfactory sex. Sometimes the sensual exercises do not have the desired outcome, however. Alongside the successful couples who transform their sex lives or at least make some palpable improvements, there are others who, through sensate focus, start to understand why they cannot realise their sexual fantasies and yearnings together. In such cases their new understanding can be a valuable if disappointing outcome, enabling a mourning process to take place and life to move on. In the case of couples for whom unconsciously or consciously intimate touch is too threatening, no change may even be a relief.

Advancing knowledge about sex

Treatments for sexual problems have come a long way since I began working as a psychotherapist in the early 1990s. Knowledge about human sexuality has grown extensively in terms of the emotional-relational and physical-biological factors contributing to sexual experience, as well as pharmacotherapies such as PDE5 inhibitors, for example Viagra, Cialis and Levitra, that fall under the banner of sexual medicine. In the 21st century, some professional training and research institutions, notably Tavistock Relationships, with its roots in 1948 post-war London, and more recently the International Psychotherapy Institute (IPI) in Washington DC, along with many seasoned practitioners, have moved towards a more integrated approach. This trend, however, is not universal. There is much still to be done.

Theories about the psychology of human relationships and human sexuality have flourished since Freud, illuminating psychotherapists' approach to couple work. A personal conviction that underpins this book is my commitment to the value of psychoanalysis as a way of understanding the complexity of human relationships and specifically the unconscious component of the multitude of sexual problems couples bring to therapy. In this respect, this book is even more a homage to psychoanalysis – and especially to Donald W Winnicott – than to Masters and Johnson's inspired intervention. However, this belief in psychoanalysis was not where I started. Following a midlife change of career from industry to therapy and gaining a diploma in individual and relationship counselling, I was awarded a second qualification, a postgraduate diploma in psychosexual therapy from the Whittington Hospital and the South Bank University, London. This diploma programme was largely based on humanistic psychotherapy, drawing on several theoretical frameworks, behavioural tools, sexual anatomy and medicine. I developed a keen interest in the medical and biological aspects of sexuality, including the impact of psychotropic drugs, illness, surgical procedures, childbirth and ageing on sexual response and the body, and had a number of papers published in professional academic journals (Pacey, 1999, 2004, 2005, 2008). Topics of these papers included the impact of the first baby on couples' sexuality, as well as female genital mutilation and circumcision.

During this my 'second' career I have found that anxieties about sex or lack of sex are often presented as the main cause of couples' and individuals' distress. In some cases, partners may feel completely mystified as to why sex is difficult. Expectations of their relationships and sexual wishes may include a seamlessness and spontaneity that are unrealisable. It may be that after years together a couple has stopped wanting sex, despite times of passionate intimacy in the past. Or it may be that sex has never been pleasurable or satisfying for one or the other partner, or both of them. Understandably these couples have a real sense of 'missing out' on an imagined joyful, bonding and exciting experience. If feeling threatened by the absence of sex, partners may become worried about each other's commitment, their security and their future together, and if young, their ability to conceive a child. The prospect of losing the relationship may feel unbearable, and fears of abandonment may emerge.

Sometimes the impact of the 'homework' (the tactile exercises done in the privacy of their home) has a complex impact on couples. Occasionally men discover their sensuality for the first time when being stroked by their partner. One of the unforgettable moments of my early professional life was when a young couple reported on their first experience of sensate focus, which had been designed ultimately to help them relax when naked in the presence of each other. Their reaction was memorable: the husband was euphoric and waxed lyrical about his own experience of touch. "Everyone should do this therapy before they get married," he declared, as he described in more detail the sheer pleasure of being caressed from head to foot by his wife and then caressing her in return. Even more interesting, I remember, was the contrast between the excited man and his rather withdrawn wife, who said little. With charm he took most of the space in his enthusiasm. Was he speaking for them both? His inquiry, "What did you think?", was met with a rather impenetrable expression on his spouse's face. She could or would not say how she was feeling, neither during the homework, nor during the therapy session. My curiosity led nowhere. What had it meant to her, I wondered, to have awakened her partner's apparently dormant sensuality? Was she delighted, unmoved or horrified by his self-discovery, and enjoying, indifferent to or dreading the prospect of being expected or asked to provide a caressing 'service' from then on? Was the homework now a threat to a more passive sexual role or sexual experience that she might have preferred? Or had *his* caressing of *her* failed to soothe her, even irritated her, stirring up aggression or unspoken anxieties about sexuality? The possible interpretations of the conscious and unconscious experience of this couple emerging at that point in the therapy were endless and to me then, mysterious. Theirs was one of many stories that became drivers in my quest to understand more about the emotional-relational forces that are activated in couples' physical intimacy, and even their anticipation of it.

Acknowledging the limitations of sex therapy

The previous vignette took place decades ago. As I became increasingly aware of the limitations of sex therapy as a couple treatment, I began to look to psychoanalysis to develop my understanding of the couple dynamics mobilised by the introduction of mutual touching exercises during therapy. My first step was in 2004 when I moved to a psychoanalytically orientated clinical supervisor. In 2010 I gained an MA in Attachment, Psychoanalysis and the Couple Relationship at Tavistock Relationships (TR), and simultaneously embarked on my personal psychoanalysis. In 2012, I joined TR's Professional Doctorate in Couple Psychotherapy programme, completed successfully in 2018. The conundrum, however, was that as my interest in psychoanalysis grew, my interest in the biomedical aspects of sexuality declined, as evidenced by my writing an editorial suggesting that the medicalisation of sex was a barrier to intercourse (Pacey, 2008). My perception was that the industry's drive to over-medicalise sexual distress was further evidence of the mind-body split in both couple relationships and in the profession of couple psychotherapy. I also noted that my clinical use of sensate focus had become infrequent. Making sense of these phenomena was a challenge. Why did one theoretical framework result in a marginalisation of the other in my practice? Why could I not be *both* a couple psychotherapist and psychosexual therapist?

At this point of awareness of the change to my practice, I decided to introduce the touching exercises with a couple who had developed the capacity for reflecting on their own material, their partner's psyche and their relationship. In a session spent by the three of us exploring the links between their experience during sensate focus and their unconscious dynamics, it was as if the tactile intervention had created a "triangular space" (Britton, 1989, p. 86) for thinking about the partners' unconscious relationship in fresh ways. Importantly, it helped the clients make illuminating connections between their emotional-relational material and their sexual problems, as well as working with the conscious physicality of their sensual-sexual pleasure and displeasure.

It is no coincidence that I designed my doctoral study to investigate how, when and why my peers working with both modalities, psychodynamic and behavioural, moved between the two approaches and how they thought about their use of sensate focus in clinical work. I wanted to find out how they made sense of their own and of their clients' experience, so that I might reflect on and arrive at a deeper understanding. My goal was to develop not only my clinical approach using the results of the study, whatever they might be, but also to influence integration in couple psychotherapy of all disciplines.

Additional factors influencing my motivation to carry out the doctoral study included the backcloth of professional fragmentation in psychosexual therapy and the general dearth of research undertaken in my profession. My own experience is that sex therapy has inadequate theoretical foundations and is at risk of professional stagnation, a view reflected by others including Kleinplatz (2003) and Binik and Meana (2009). Kleinplatz also makes the point that the focus of sexual medicine remains the alleviation of symptoms rather than enhanced sexual relations. In the same paper, she criticises the psychoanalytic approach for being costly and time-intensive. I would add that anecdotal evidence suggests that contemporary psychotherapy and sensate focus both seem to suffer from misunderstandings and misconceptions *within* the profession as well as outside it (Levine, 2009; Berry, 2014). These realities support the argument for greater theoretical integration of mind, body and relationship in couple psychotherapy, particularly when sex is the main presenting issue.

Recognising sensate focus as one element of sex therapy

Several themes permeating this book contribute to the debate. Before describing these, an important digression needs to be made. Some participants in my 2018 study reminded me that psychosexual therapy offers much more than sensate focus, and they were right. Sex therapy offers numerous behavioural tools and exercises to treat common sexual dysfunctions, including problems with erections, ejaculation and orgasm, sexual interest and arousal disorder, genito-pelvic pain and penetration disorder and many more; there are techniques for minimising anxiety, relaxing and focusing; there are ways of building body awareness, alleviating negative body image, teaching arousal circuits and basic sexual anatomy, and finally offering essential sexual information. All these tools may help demystify sex and promote clients' sexual confidence. Living in highly sexualised western societies, where sexual articles, stories and images abound on the streets and across the media and the internet, couples may find it difficult to navigate through the sea of sexual messages. This is especially true of clients who have been raised in environments and cultures where discussion of sex and of sexual relationships is taboo. Unfortunately more openness and proliferation of information about sex do not necessarily lead to greater relationship and sexual happiness: witness the continuous spate of stories of sexual harassment between adults, adolescents and even children (Woolcock, 2021) that are regularly reported in the UK press. Add to this the negative influence and pressures of bullying in social media. These create fears of failure and fantasies based on impossible expectations of sex both of oneself and of any partner. For the younger generations, this increasing trend seems counterproductive to learning about healthy relationships and expressing sexual desire and satisfaction with another complex human being. Further exploration of the topic of sexual bullying and harassment and the role of education is beyond the scope of this book. However, such phenomena are damaging to the individual, the family and society.

Eschewing the notion of a panacea

Returning now to the themes that thread through this book, an important point is that sensate focus is not a panacea. Practitioners who have been well trained in its use know that it is helpful in clinical work to widely varying degrees and that it is not for universal application. A reflective and ethical psychotherapist considers carefully over time her own motivation for introducing a prescriptive tool into the therapy, and especially the influence of the countertransference field, as well as the possible dynamics that might be mobilised in the clients as a result. Sensate focus has its limitations as well as its powers; the former were respected by the trainers and supervisors I interviewed. Indeed their comments took me back to my early psychosexual therapy training, when I recall overhearing a senior tutor chastising two trainees for having introduced sensate focus during their first session with a particular couple. While learning from mistakes is part of anyone's training and part of a therapist's continuing professional development, that scenario is a valuable memory, since the question of when, not only whether, to use this intervention is a moot point. The way I think about sensate focus now is a million miles away from those early clinical encounters, when prescribing the tactile exercises within weeks of the first consultation was an acceptable strategy. Today I might broach the topic with clients only after months of engagement, or possibly a year, or even longer, or not at all. If I introduce the concept earlier, I need to have thought through my reasons for doing so and carefully assessed any risk. That said, some couples may put significant pressure on their therapist to start "working directly on sex", as they see it, and clients' anxieties driving that pressure may be complex. Importantly these anxieties are likely to be felt in the countertransference as the therapist's own helplessness and a sense of not knowing what to do. The 'if and when' of sensate focus is a judgement call for every clinician and this book is intended to provide ideas to assist practitioners in their clinical *reflections*, rather than their clinical actions.

Focusing on process

One of the key messages of this book is that the tactile exercises need to be understood as a *process*, not a programme. It is a couple's emotional responses to each task that inform the therapist of partners' anxieties about sexuality and the developmental repairs that need to take place. Set out on paper as a step-by-step, two-phased programme, the exercises may seem simple. Perhaps this mistaken perception is born of the original design by Masters and Johnson, which was a behavioural programme that excluded the emotional-relational world of their clients and therapists alike. Maybe this perception permeates the countless versions to be found online. Occasionally during history-taking or at an early stage of their therapy, couples report unsolicited how they discovered sensate focus on the internet, tried it and found it unhelpful. A psychotherapist might well be curious about the myriad factors and dynamics potentially underpinning these sexual stories. Be that as it may, sensate focus is not a tool that can used effectively by couples alone without the framework and safety that therapy provides. This is because on the whole partners with problems cannot talk about their experience with each other and trying to solve sexual problems without professional help is likely to leave their relationship unchanged. A few times in the past, couples have asked for a written copy of the tactile exercises. Interestingly no client having received this information, all contained on one side of an A4 sheet of paper, has ever read the content. Could it be that in the transference, having the information to hand and making the future tasks 'predictable' restores a sense of control in some couples' minds?

To a certain extent the successful introduction of sensate focus in couple psychotherapy depends on the 'comfort zone' of the practitioner in matters of sex and sexuality. Not all psychotherapists of any paradigm, including couple therapists, are skilled or willing to delve into this intimate, private arena of human experience. Not every practitioner feels confident and competent when invited to explore clients' sexual material or even discuss the affective component of sexual relationships. The sudden awareness of this possibility about my own professional group came many years after I qualified as a psychotherapist. Up until then I had believed that all my peers who were psychosexual therapists were able to work with sexuality. Sex was after all the currency of the training we had all had. In recent years, however, I have discovered that this is not the case. When undertaking my research and attending professional gatherings, I have learned that a psychosexual therapy qualification does not necessarily indicate a willingness to talk in detail about sex. Mostly it does, but not in absolutely every case. Surprised by this new finding about my profession, I shared it with a long-term colleague who listened in total disbelief. It was hard for her to hear and to her mind incredible. To be fair, meeting a psychotherapist qualified in sex therapy who is not at ease discussing sex is a rare event. Perhaps for some therapists who may not have resolved their Oedipal complex, unconscious anxieties about merger and exclusion are mobilised when working with sexual relationships; or their need to avoid the intrinsic discomfort of intrusion into a primal relationship is compelling. Perhaps the message from this story is that in my experience, therapists who are not comfortable in the sexual zone usually acknowledge this limitation in their work and act appropriately by referring couples who are sexually unhappy elsewhere.

Similarly not every psychotherapist is open to the concept of sensate focus and many objections are raised concerning its use in clinical practice. Traditional psychoanalysts are a case in point: for this group, such a concrete intervention is directive and prescriptive and flies in the face of working in the transference. In addition, practitioners specialising in, say, same-sex couples or those with particular sexual preferences, or couples of different ethnicities, may reject sensate focus as a normative tool, alien to their clients' worldview. It may be argued that sensate focus, designed as it was decades ago and conceived as a residential programme at The Masters and Johnson Institute for predominantly white, middle class, educated, wealthy, heterosexual couples, is out of kilter with social diversity in the 21st century. In response to these claims, I would assert that the need to touch and be touched is universal in human nature: just consider how much bodily contact any healthy mother and baby share, even if for some unfortunate children and adults, early trauma makes it hard to express and fulfil that need later in life. Whatever the sociocultural milieu, sexuality and gender of a couple presenting for treatment, sensate focus needs to be custom-designed by a therapist who is curious about and sensitive to the partners' unique experience, psychopathology and relationship.

Clarifying terms used in this book

Using terms interchangeably

Throughout this book some terms are used interchangeably, since there is often debate but no consensus on their definition. This strategy on terminology is intended principally to create variety for the reader. Terms used interchangeably, unless otherwise specified, include:

- *psychosexual therapy* and *sex therapy*
- *sexual and relationship psychotherapist, psychosexual therapist* and *sex therapist*
- *couple psychotherapy, couple therapy* and *couple work*
- *psychodynamic couple psychotherapist, couple psychotherapist* and *couple therapist*
- *psychotherapist, analyst, therapist, clinician* and *practitioner*
- *sexual dysfunction, sexual disorder, sexual problem* and *sexual difficulty.*

For brevity, variety and convenience, the term 'homework' is also used as a synonym for sensate focus exercises throughout the book. However, any sense of obligation or expectation conveyed by the term is unintended. Nevertheless, some clients might consciously or unconsciously perceive the exercises as an unwelcome task or chore, or they may relate to it as the hoped-for solution to their problem.

The term 'client' is used throughout in preference to the term 'patient', which carries medical associations.

Using gendered pronouns

Since much of the discussion of psychoanalytic theory in this book refers to the mother-infant dyad, generally the pronoun 'she' is used to denote the mother and the pronoun 'he' to denote the infant or child. This is for the sake of clarity for the reader and is not intended to imply a theoretical focus on male babies, nor that biological mothers are universally the main caregivers of infants. As most psychotherapists in the UK are female, the pronoun 'she' is also used when referring generally to therapists and 'he' is used when discussing hypothetical clients; 'he' or 'she' is used as appropriate when discussing the clinical vignettes of individual male and female participants in my doctoral study.

The case vignettes drawn from research interviews explicitly included heterosexual and same-sex couples, male and female. Participants in my study did not specify other LGBTQIA+ clients, that is people who describe themselves as bisexual, trans, or queer or any other non-heteronormative term regarding sexual orientation and gender.

References

Berry, M.D. (2014) *Towards a psychodynamically-informed model for the integrative psychotherapeutic treatment of male sexual dysfunction.* PhD thesis, University College London [Online]. https://ethos.bl.uk (Accessed: 3 February 2016).

Binik, Y.M. and Meana, M. (2009) 'The future of sex therapy: Specialization or marginalization?', *Archives of Sexual Behavior*, 38(6), pp. 1016–1027. https://doi.org/10.1007/s10508-009-9475-9

Britton, R. (1989) 'The missing link: parental sexuality in the Oedipus complex', in Steiner, J. (ed.) *The Oedipus complex today.* London: Karnac, pp. 83–102.

Caruso, N. (2011) 'The entangled nature of attachment and sexuality in the couple relationship', *Couple and Family Psychoanalysis*, 1(1), pp. 117–135.

Giraldi, A. and Graziottin, A. (2007) 'Sexual arousal disorders in women', in Porst, H. and Buvat, J. (eds.) *Standard practice in sexual medicine.* Malden, MT: Blackwell, pp. 325–333.

Green, L. and Seymour, J. (2009) 'Loss of desire: A psychosexual case study', in Clulow, C. (ed.) *Sex, attachment and couple psychotherapy.* London: Karnac, pp. 141–163.

Kaplan, H.S. (1974) *The new sex therapy.* New York: Times Books.

Kaplan, H.S. (1987) *The illustrated manual of sex therapy.* 2nd edn. New York: Brunner Mazel.

Kleinplatz, P.J. (2003) 'What's new in sex therapy? From stagnation to fragmentation', *Sexual and Relationship Therapy*, 18(1), pp. 95–106. https://doi.org/10.1080/1468199031000061290

Levine, S.B. (2009) 'I am not a sex therapist!', *Archives of Sexual Behavior*, 38(6), pp. 1033–1034. https://doi.org/10.1007/s10508-009-9474-x

Masters, W.H. and Johnson, V.E. (1970) *Human sexual inadequacy.* Boston: Little, Brown & Co.

Pacey, S. (1999) 'Torture, transformation or treatment? Ethics and physical interventions to the sexual self', *Sexual and Marital Therapy*, 14(3), pp. 255–275. https://doi.org/10.1080/02674659908405411

Pacey, S. (2004) 'Couples and the first baby: Responding to new parents' sexual and relationship problems', *Sexual and Relationship Therapy*, 19(3), pp. 223–246. https://doi.org/10.1080/14681990410001715391

Pacey, S. (2005) 'Step change: The interplay of sexual and parenting problems when couples form stepfamilies', *Sexual and Relationship Therapy*, 20(3), pp. 359–369. https://doi.org/10.1080/14681990500141899

Pacey, S. (2008) 'The medicalisation of sex: A barrier to intercourse?', *Sexual and Relationship Therapy*, 23(3), pp. 183–188. https://doi.org/10.1080/14681990802221092

Pacey, S.L. (2018) *An investigation into psychodynamic couple psychotherapists' theories of sensate focus in clinical work.* DCplPsych thesis, University of East London, London [Online]. https://ethos.bl.uk/OrderDetails.do?did=1&uin=uk.bl.ethos.775621 (Accessed: 1 March 2020).

Parker, C. (2003) The distance (A kiss with string attached) 2003 [Exhibit]. *Tate Britain*, 1 June.

Rey, H. (1994) *Universals of psychoanalysis in the treatment of psychotic and borderline states*. London: Free Association.

Riley, A. (2007) 'Commentary on Rowland's article', *Journal of Sex & Marital Therapy*, 33(5), pp. 461–466. https://doi.org/10.1080/00926230701480422

Rosen, R.C. (2007) 'Erectile dysfunction. Integration of medical and psychological approaches', in Leiblum, S.R. (ed.) *Principles and practice of sex therapy*. 4th edn. New York: The Guilford Press.

Scharff, D.E. and Savege Scharff, J. (1991) *Object relations couple therapy*. London: Jason Aronson.

Weiner, L. and Avery-Clark, C. (2017) *Sensate focus in sex therapy. The illustrated manual*. Abingdon: Routledge.

Woolcock, N. (2021) 'Mobiles banned to curb sexual bullying at school', *The Times*, 15 June. https://www.thetimes.co.uk/article/mobile-phones-banned-to-curb-sexual-bullying-at-school-khv69jv0m

Chapter 2

Splitting

Separating mind, body and relationship

The predominant psychological treatments for sexual problems in the UK and probably elsewhere are based, broadly speaking, on two separate schools of thought: couple psychotherapy and psychosexual therapy. In the latter, sexual symptoms are interpreted as somatic phenomena in the individual, usually requiring a diagnosis such as delayed ejaculation or orgasmic disorder. The psychosexual therapist's clinical focus is on partners' conscious feelings, sensations and physical interaction of a sensual and sexual nature, with a less overt exploration of the couple's unconscious dynamics or interaction. For the sex therapist, a detailed, illuminating history, including sexual experience and functioning, of each spouse is standard procedure and fundamental to her formulation of the couple. Usually one of the partners presents as the 'patient' with, say, erectile disorder or sexual pain. As the 'non-symptomatic' partner has an equal role in maintaining the problem, the question is this: does the therapist think about and seek to understand the couple's unconscious contract that maintains their sexual symptoms, or is the contract at risk of being overlooked?

By contrast, in couple psychotherapy therapists tend either to avoid talking about sex (Kahr, 2009), or to think about sexuality in metaphorical and symbolic terms, interpreting common problems such as erectile difficulties as manifestations of shared somatised defences to ward off emotional-relational anxieties. Colman (2009, p. 46) suggests that the couple psychotherapist "interprets away from" sex and seeks to understand the meaning of a physical symptom in one partner in terms of the couple's relatedness to the object. Sex is therefore more likely to be seen as a stepping stone into the emotional world of the couple, not as a bodily sexual relationship that also needs care. The couple psychotherapist focuses on the sea of unconscious processes operating between spouses at any time, and much less, if at all, on the partners' conscious sexual-physical dissatisfaction. This paradigm begs the question: how much does the psychotherapist's avoidance of talking about sex reflect her own unconscious anxiety?

An example of this difference between psychodynamic and psychosexual approaches may be gleaned from Grier's (2001, p. 201) notion of "no sex" couples. In

DOI: 10.4324/9781003328292-2

his chapter, Grier offers clinical vignettes of three couples and writes a fascinating and convincing account of his endeavours to understand and help them through the Freudian theory of the Oedipus complex. From Grier's clinical material the reader grasps that his definition of no sex is firstly, a couple who have sex sporadically but not regularly; secondly, a couple who have had a good sexual relationship in the past but not resumed sex after childbirth; and thirdly, a couple who have an ongoing satisfying sex life. Interestingly this third couple disclose that they have regular, good sex only several months into the therapy. In psychosexual therapy, such a fact would probably emerge at the start of therapy during the history-taking of the clients' lives and sexual experience. Another difference between the two paradigms is that in sex therapy Grier's couples might not be regarded as no sex. That said, would the psychosexual therapist be trained to identify and resolve partners' Oedipal anxieties using Grier's method?

On reading this distinction between theoretical approaches, many sex therapists would probably protest that they *do* work with the unconscious, and they have a point; indisputably the unconscious is everywhere and operates in every therapy session conducted under the banner of any paradigm. The point here is whether or not the psychosexual clinician is reflecting on and understanding couples' unconscious processes, anxieties and defences that are mobilised by engaging in and talking about sex and sensate focus. On the other hand, is the couple psychotherapist willing to help clients with the *physical* aspects of sex? For example, a successful psychodynamic therapy treatment might leave partners happier, more differentiated, more open and more communicative but still unable to share sensual or sexual play. If the couple are disappointed not to have resumed sex, is that explored? Without recourse to a tool such as sensate focus, what does the couple psychotherapist do in such circumstances?

Losing sex in psychoanalysis

These observations on the separation of mind and body raise several issues, taking the reader back in time to early treatments for sexual problems and to Freudian thought. Sigmund Freud (1912, p. 183) asserted, from a premise that is now commonly perceived as a theory of male sexuality, that more or less all men suffer from psychical impotence:

Where they love they do not desire and where they desire they cannot love.

In his claim that the fate of all men is to separate physically and mentally the two different currents of sex and affection, Freud created the original formulation of psychic splitting. During the first half of the 20th century until the late 1960s, Freud's influence in the field of sexual medicine was pervasive: most clinicians treating sexual problems were psychiatrists working within a Freudian model (Berry, 2013). His major theories of infantile sexuality, three-phase (oral, anal and genital) sexual development and the Oedipus complex provided psychogenic explanations for sexual problems (Freud, 1905). Famously, Freud (1923, p. 26) acknowledged the inseparability of mind and body in his widely quoted comment that "the ego is first and foremost a bodily ego," adding that "the ego is ultimately derived by bodily sensations, chiefly from those springing from the surface of the body . . . representing the superficies of the mental apparatus". It is clear from this claim that he linked sensations of the body surface to ego integration, which for Freud was fundamental to healthy mental development.

Exploring the mind-body connection in Freudian theory, Colman (2009) suggests that the notion of libido was conceived by Freud as a bridge between psyche and soma as he sought to discover a physical basis for psychic life. Libido, suggests Colman, was a sophisticated form of the sexual instinct and the driver of psychological organisation. In Freud's view (1917, p. 258), libidinal energy was the psychic equivalent of the impulse in the neurone; he did not know how the transition was made from body to mind and vice versa, only that he had observed this phenomenon in clinical work. He referred to it as a "puzzling leap", re-named the "mysterious leap" by Deutsch (1957, p. 160), a phrase that to this day is widely credited to Freud, not Deutsch. Freud understood adult sexual symptoms as indicators of underlying neuroses and psychopathology, stemming from interference in early psychosexual development and unresolved Oedipal dilemmas. His treatment for sexual dysfunction was psychoanalysis; in other words, he targeted the mind, not the body, or at least not directly.

Before and during Freud's pre-eminent period of the early decades of the 1900s, a number of esteemed thinkers provided an important backcloth of sexual science for his theories. Among these theorists was psychiatrist Richard von Krafft-Ebing (1886), whose major work, *Psychopathia Sexualis*, described many of the scientific assumptions about sex of the time and contributed greatly to the late 19th century discourse on pathological psychosexual conditions. According to Waldinger (2008), sexology was developed mainly at this time by German psychiatrists at Berlin's famous Institut für Sexualwissenschaft (Institute for Sexual Research) until 1933, when it was destroyed by the Nazis. Outstanding scholars of the era also included British physician, Henry Havelock Ellis (1897–1928), who produced *Studies in the Psychology of Sex*, a six-volume encyclopaedia of human sexual biology, behaviour and attitudes. Ellis' work represented a significant advance in sexual science, extending the application of psychology to sexual dysfunction and fostering greater social openness about sex.

In the aftermath of World War II, interest in sexology was revived in the United States, now by non-medically trained scientists, among whom was biologist and sexual statistician, Alfred Kinsey (Waldinger, 2008). Kinsey (1948, 1953) and his colleagues conducted the first large-scale surveys of American sexual behaviour. Kinsey's reports shocked the nation with his findings of widespread masturbation, extramarital affairs and homosexuality, provoking a sexual revolution despite fierce opposition from "the guardians of American morality" (Sheldon, 2008, p. 22). A decade or more later, when Masters and Johnson (1966) published the results of their 11-year study of sex, *Human Sexual Response*, triggering the publication of a range of behavioural treatments in a book entitled *Human Sexual Inadequacy* (1970), they did so amid a sociocultural wave of freedom and permissiveness following the sexual liberation era of the 1960s. The new ideals of this revolution proclaimed "spontaneity, sensuality and rejection of restrictive inhibitions" and a "liberation of the body" (Goodwach, 2005, p. 157). However, in the late 1980s, when celebrated sex therapist Kaplan (1987, p. 17) made references to "our sexually repressed society", it is possible that she was highlighting the co-existence of widely varying attitudes and psychosocial mores affecting sexuality and sexual practices in the United States at that time, attitudes that in the 21st century seem to continue in the multicultural western world.

Reconciling Freud and couple therapy

By the 1970s, as Masters and Johnson's behavioural therapies gained momentum and popularity, most psychiatrists of the 1950s and 1960s who had trained in psychoanalysis lost interest in treating patients with sexual disorders (Waldinger, 2008). One eminent practitioner, however, succeeded in combining Freudian analytic thinking with the new bodily approaches in her clinical work. This was Helen Singer Kaplan, a psychiatrist and psychoanalyst with a keen interest in behavioural science, who pioneered an integrated psychoanalytic-behavioural sex therapy in the 1970s and led the field for two decades until her death in 1995 (Saxon, 1995). Interestingly the later theories and practices of both Masters and Johnson (Kolodny, 1981) and Kaplan (1995) suggest that they would only treat sexual problems within a couple framework. Currently this is not the case in the UK, where offering clients the option of individual or couple treatments for sexual dysfunction is common in psychosexual therapy. Anecdotal evidence is that sensate focus does not help a couple when only one partner is in treatment, for reasons discussed later in this book.

Kaplan's published work remains an important training resource in sex therapy today (Goodwach, 2005). Her ascendancy coincided with psychoanalysis' apparently declining interest in sex, as object relations and the mother-infant dyad replaced Freudian libido and the three-person sexual rivalries of the Oedipus complex as the principal paradigm (Fonagy, 2009). The move away from Freud in the UK was largely due to the powerful influence of Melanie Klein, whose theories and practice took the Oedipus complex away from the heterosexuality of parents and the innate drive of young children to displace the opposite-sex parent, to a much earlier phase, that is, infancy, and the infant's developmental challenge of integrating the loved and hated breast. Within Klein's model, infant sexuality was present and acknowledged, but no longer central to the baby's psyche and psychological organisation. An equally eminent psychoanalytic theorist, Donald Winnicott, who was also a paediatrician, held that good enough maternal care in the earliest months of life was the critical factor in healthy human maturation and, if received, the infant would certainly be capable of navigating his way successfully through the Oedipus complex at a later stage.

Medicalising sex

In the mid-1990s, after Kaplan, the behavioural and biological aspects of sexual performance became the treatment target of pharmaceutical companies who "suddenly realized the enormous potential financial consequences of sexual-enhancing drugs for mass consumption" (Waldinger, 2007, p. 35), exemplifying a prevailing reductionist view of sexual distress in the industry (Rowland, 2007). In the late 20th century, however, disenchantment with the limitations of behavioural techniques was emerging within the sex therapy field and this was compounded by a new, growing awareness of the more complex aetiology of sexual difficulties (LoPiccolo, 1994). These factors, combined with a backlash against the symptom-focused pharmacological treatment model epitomised by Viagra (Tiefer, 2006; Waldinger, 2008), led to the conception of a biopsychosocial paradigm for treating sexual disorders (McCabe et al., 2010). Importantly, pharmacotherapy's possible threat to the place of psychotherapy in the treatment of sexual problems did not materialise (DeRogatis, 2007; Rowland, 2007). Instead, a continuing place for psychotherapies targeting sexual disorders was confirmed, despite the lack of evidence-based studies in this field (Waldinger, 2015). Moreover, there has been renewed interest in sex in the field of psychoanalysis and psychodynamic couple psychotherapy (Fonagy, 2009). A more detailed history of the relationship between psychoanalysis and sex therapy is outside the scope of this book. However, the interested reader will find full accounts of this topic in Goodwach (2005), Waldinger (2007, 2008) and Berry (2013, 2014).

Conceiving psychodynamic couple psychotherapy

Counselling wartime couples and families

Psychodynamic couple psychotherapy in the UK dates back to 1948 when Enid Balint (then Eichholz) founded the Family Discussion Bureau (FDB), which was renamed periodically over the decades and is today Tavistock Relationships (TR) in London. The original purpose of the FDB, an offshoot of the Family Welfare Association and supported by senior psychoanalysts at the Tavistock Clinic, was to study problem marriages and train caseworkers to counsel couples and displaced, traumatised families in London in the aftermath of World War II (Bannister et al., 1955). As a welfare worker and subsequently a psychoanalyst, Balint recognised the pivotal role of the marital dyad in the emotional security of family life and understood the centrality of unconscious as well as conscious motivations in spouses' ways of relating (Sutherland, 1954). Balint (1968) also acknowledged the central role of sex in couple interaction. The FDB's development of a psychodynamic approach to couple therapy was elaborated in three early books (Bannister et al., 1955, 1960; Bannister & Pincus, 1965). The interested reader will find a detailed account of the history of the organisational network within which TR came into being in Clulow et al. (2018) and Balfour (2021).

Soon after the founding of the FDB, circa 1949, Henry Dicks was also conducting studies of marriage within a specialist unit in the adult department of the Tavistock Clinic, London. The results of his unit's research were published extensively in the 1950s and culminated in the publication of Dicks' book, *Marital Tensions* in 1967. Sexual problems such as non-consummation of marriage, maintained jointly by the woman's fear and the man's early ejaculation ("ejaculatio praecox"), were treated as "the dyadic presenting symptomatology", that is their shared unconscious anxieties and collusion in marrying "on an anti-libidinal basis" (Dicks, 1967, pp. 152–153). Dicks clearly addressed a wide range of sexual "disturbances" in couples observed through the lens of Fairbairn-Klein object relations.

The key point here is that by the mid-1960s, the marital dyad had become a focus of research and psychotherapeutic action in its own right. These two units, the social work-oriented FDB and the relationally and medically oriented marital group in the Tavistock, were the platform for subsequent developments in couple psychotherapy. Evolving theories from the two research-based centres illuminated the dynamic tension between individual development and the couple relationship throughout the life cycle. In the 21st century, the psychosocial and political consequences of marriage or partnership breakdown, especially its impact on children, remain an acknowledged challenge to society (Kahr, 2012).

To advance their understanding of the psychological functioning of couples, Balint, Dicks and their contemporaries drew on 'cutting edge' Kleinian theories of the infant-mother relationship, namely the baby's use of his mother as an internal object, and projective and introjective identification (Ruszyzynski, 1993a). Balint's group were strongly influenced not only by Kleinian object relations, but also by other eminent object relations theorists, including Winnicott, Michael Balint, Fairbairn and later, Bowlby. The development of the object relations school in the UK since the 1930s made a subtle but profound shift in the understanding of human behaviour by moving away from Freudian instinct theory, as described earlier, focusing instead on the mother-baby unit and seeing the individual as primarily motivated to seek relationships.

Understanding the couple relationship: fundamental concepts

By the 1990s, under the banner of the Tavistock Marital Studies Institute (TMSI), psychoanalytic-psychodynamic theories of couple relationships and clinical practice grew in sophistication thanks to the post-Kleinians. Since then, there has been a strong dependence on Kleinian object relations and it is debatable whether this dependency illustrates a non-sexual reading of human development in couple work. Be that as it may, consider the central tenet of psychoanalysis and couple psychotherapy, which is that human behaviour and experience are driven by unconscious as much as, if not more than, conscious motivations. Internal object relations, formed in the earliest months, are unconscious and influence powerfully how adult couples behave, think and respond to each other:

> From the very beginning, the infant is a subject taking the mother as his object of attachment. But the mother in her own right is also a subject and takes the infant as her object of care and concern. A complex interaction, therefore, goes on between the two, and within that, adaptive and defensive processes of each are geared in with those of the other and have to function in relation to the other (Bannister & Pincus, 1965). The nature of this first object relation becomes a prototype for all subsequent childhood and adult relationships.
>
> (Ruszczynski, 1993a, p. 200)

As this quotation suggests, in the intensity and intimacy of long-term adult sexual relationships, partners reconnect with their infantile experience, positive and negative, and re-enact their object relations in their daily verbal and nonverbal interaction (Ruszczynski, 1992). From the 1990s and for three decades, TR, formerly TMSI, sought to understand couples' interaction in terms of key Kleinian concepts, including the two Kleinian developmental positions, which are the paranoid-schizoid and the depressive constellations; projective and introjective identification; the marital fit and the unconscious contract; and transference and countertransference (Ruszczynski, 1993b).

Today in the 2020s, Morgan (2019) has updated TR's model for couple psychotherapy, drawing on Ruszczynski's paradigm, Britton's (1989, p. 88) notion of the "third area" and three-person, triangular relationships, and Morgan's own wealth of clinical experience. Echoing the 2019 book's title, the contemporary TR therapist is trained to hold a "couple state of mind", which entails relating to the partners from a third position as observer of their interaction (Morgan, 2019, pp. 184–185). The therapist's aim is to enable the couple to internalise this state of mind, so that they develop the capacity to think about their own and each other's perspective, and about the relationship they create together. In this way they become an analytic couple. This latter concept applies when the partners develop a reflective capacity and can think about themselves and their relationship creatively in the absence of the therapist. Under these circumstances they are able to use their relationship as a daily resource and especially in times of stress when negotiating life's challenges and changes.

Rethinking projective identification as a couple strategy

Klein's (1946) concept of projective and introjective identification is the mainstay of contemporary couple psychotherapy. Initially regarded as a (shared) defence, projective identification emanated from Klein's (1946) discovery of schizoid mechanisms operating in primitive life. In adult couples, these forces continue to operate unconsciously, with each partner acting as a repository for the other's projections. Choice of partner is based partly on an individual's need for a fitting receptacle for his projections and disowned aspects of self, which may be loved, rejected or criticised by the other. Good parts of the self may be projected into the other for "safekeeping, if felt to be threatened by the bad inside" (Morgan, 2019, p. 89). The receptiveness of each partner to the other's projections is the couple's "marital fit", which "consists of shared phantasies and shared defences" (Ruszczynski, 1992, p. 36). Operating on an unconscious contract, which has both developmental and defensive possibilities, spouses respond or react to the other's needs and together achieve a kind of homeostasis, a dynamic but limiting and limited shift between satisfaction and conflict or tension (Balint, 1968). Thus the couple psychotherapist focuses on the ways in which the unconscious, internal worlds of two partners dovetail with and mutually influence one another (Balint, 1968), and considers how defensive, dysfunctional or collusive their shared anxieties and defences seem to be.

When assessing couples, Morgan (2019, p. 4) considers first how potentially developmental or defensive they are, and secondly their "psychic development" in becoming a couple. Here critical factors include their relationship to the primary object, their working through the Oedipal situation and adolescent experience. Couples' dynamics operating in the present, while rooted in the past, are often about separateness, intimacy or dependency, all grouped by Morgan as part of partners' shared unconscious phantasies about the meaning of being a couple, and the unconscious beliefs and expectations that drive their patterns of relating often in dysfunctional ways.

If blaming and harsh behaviour predominates, a couple's shared internal object relations may be markedly distorting their perceptions of the external world, including their partner, leading to excessive defensiveness or idealisation and denigration in their relationship. This type of relating is typical of the paranoid-schizoid position, which is characterised by persecutory phantasies. As the relationship with the therapist grows, couples may become more capable of relating in the depressive position. At these moments, by talking about and interpreting the couple's dysfunctional ways of relating, the psychotherapist helps the couple become conscious of and understand their "unconscious manoeuvrings" (Ruszczynski, 1992, p. 40). These interventions enable the couple to take back and own their projections and modify the ways they interact:

> By locating the split-off parts and disowned aspects of the self in the other, the partner has the opportunity to live close to that which has been felt to be unmanageable. . . . In doing this each partner modifies the internal world of the other and allows the other to move towards a greater degree of integration.
>
> (Ruszczynski, 1992, p. 37)

Understanding the paranoid-schizoid and depressive constellations

Klein's notion of two constellations of mental development, the paranoid-schizoid and the depressive positions, are at the core of couple psychotherapy. The paranoid-schizoid position concerns the anxieties of the infant's first months of life and his primitive object relations, that is, to part-objects such as the breast, or a hand, but not yet to the whole mother as a person. The baby is striving to cope with his innate life and death instincts, as well as the good, loving exchanges and the bad, rejecting experiences with his mother or environment (Ruszczynski, 1992). The defences developed during this phase of growth are splitting off and projecting the anxiety-making experience, along with parts of the self. The latter risk becoming disowned by the individual, limiting his potential development and his relationships as he grows (Ruszczynski, 1993b).

In the depressive position, evolving in the second half of the first year, the baby's capacity to manage both good and bad experiences with his mother is more developed and he begins to understand that the object of his love and hate is the same person, and that he himself is capable of both emotions. As a result, he feels guilt and concern that his hate might damage his loved and needed caregiver, leading to his loss of her (Ruszczynski, 1993b). The nature of his anxiety at this point is depressive and a healthy ambivalence emerges, which is regarded in Kleinian psychoanalysis as the beginning of integration and psychological maturity. Integration is never wholly achieved by any human being; movement between the two Kleinian positions is lifelong. In adulthood therefore stressful and traumatic events tend to propel partners back into paranoid-schizoid anxieties and defences, in which conflict and blame predominate and may not be managed or resolved by the couple alone. Dysfunctional couples presenting for therapy are likely to be operating mostly in the paranoid-schizoid position. A positive therapeutic outcome for such clients might be the partners' increased capacity to relate in the depressive position and therefore in psychologically healthier ways. Couples' oscillation between the two positions, between more mature and primitive ways of relating, is inevitable and can be developmental when the couple form new views and theories that are whole-object-based and result in "creative thinking and living", moving to a "post-depressive position, in other words, a new one" (Morgan, 2019, p. 135). The ultimate achievement, which some couples reach, is a

> creative couple state of mind . . . in which . . . [the couple] increases the capacity to think together, in a way they could not do, each on their own. This becomes an internal capacity, an 'internal creative couple' in the *individual*.
>
> (p. 184)

Identifying couple transference and countertransference

Transference and countertransference are concepts fundamental in understanding couple dynamics and in psychoanalytic technique. Transference, that is, feelings about early life figures (usually but not always parents) that are transferred unconsciously to the partner or psychotherapist, is fundamental in understanding couple dynamics. Transference operates in partners' daily interactions, which are often unspoken and conveyed in facial expression, gestures or in other body language (Balint, 1968). Transference also underpins couples' unrealistic hopes, expectations, wishes and fears about their partnership (Balint, 1968). In couple psychotherapy, it is the "marital transference", that is, the couple's "shared internal images and object relations, which determines partners' shared concept of being 'a couple'" (Ruszczynski, 1992, p. 40). The therapist's interpretation of the marital transference is the primary tool for bringing about change in couple dynamics.

The use of countertransference, that is, the responses evoked in the therapist during a session, is also an essential tool in couple psychotherapy, as discussed later in this book. Using her countertransference means that the therapist remains alert to her feelings and how she is reacting to the patient during the therapy hour. This modern definition of countertransference has evolved significantly since Freud's (1910) first use of the term as the analyst's unconscious resistance to exploring aspects of the patient's psychopathology that were problematic in the analyst's own psyche. With advances in psychoanalytic theory, including Paula Heimann's (1950) seminal paper *On Countertransference*, Wilfred Bion's (1962) concept of container-contained and Betty Joseph's (1985) idea of the total transference operating in the therapy room, definitions of countertransference have been open to debate for decades (Laplanche & Pontalis, 1983). In couple psychotherapy, the therapist's subjective experience is thought to be a symptom of primitive projective identification processes (described earlier) operating at the time, and is seen not only as the client's defence mechanisms, but also as an unconscious communication from couple to therapist. The proposition is that the "recipient of the projective identification is affected by it, such that he can experience whatever is projected into him" (Carpy, 1989, p. 288). From this perspective, the couple provoke their expected relational responses in the therapist, who consciously contains that which has been projected by the partners, reflects on and detoxifies it, as described in Bion's (1962) concept of the mother's rêverie. The clients can then re-ingest, digest and process the experience, which has become manageable.

Another perspective is that the countertransference is at least partially the therapist's own transference to the couple. For this reason, maintaining awareness of her subjective self and tapping into her psychological self-knowledge are a constant challenge to the therapist. The dynamics of a session are never 'pure', never 'either or', but muddied and messy. The analyst needs to remain open to self-observation as well as observing the client couple, taking cues from all parties and remaining internally integrated, interpreting material in a way that fits the unfolding therapeutic process. In all these ways the therapist's use of her subjective self can be developmental for the couple. Crucial to professional competence in the use of countertransference, however, is the psychotherapist's own psychoanalysis. As Morgan (2019, p. 78) asserts, we need to understand "the analytic process from the inside out as it is not an experience that can just be taught, it has also to have been had". Undoubtedly psychotherapists working with adult sexual relationships need to have undergone their own analysis. The question is whether therapists learn about their own sexuality during their own analysis and become comfortable discussing sexual issues, an achievement that would enable them to explore, understand and contain clients' anxieties about sexuality with competence and confidence.

Theorising about sex

Debatably this summary illustrates a lack of direct theorising about sex in couple psychotherapy. Ultimately do all of the brilliant Kleinian and other concepts described previously fail to capture or think about human psychosexual development? Historically the type of intercourse that couple psychotherapy seems to have addressed is at an unconscious level, with projection and introjection of psychic content standing in for sex and the intermingling of bodily fluids. As part of my doctoral study, I scanned 13 landmark books on theory and practice from the FDB, TMSI and TR between 1955 and 2014, and concluded that authors' interest in couples' sexuality is sporadic. In some books, sex is virtually omitted: for example, in Mattinson and Sinclair (1979), Ruszczynski (1993b), Ruszczynski and Fisher (1995), Fisher (1999) and Clulow (2001). By contrast, in others such as Bannister et al. (1960), a wide variety of sexual issues from dislike of sexual intercourse to sexual anxieties in childhood are featured. Five decades later Clulow (2009), Clulow and Boerma (2009), Green and Seymour (2009) and Caruso (2014a) provide book chapters about couples' sexual relationships and include psychosexual therapy to address the physicality of adult sex.

The most recent text expounding the Tavistock Relationships' model for the psychoanalysis of couples, *A Couple State of Mind*, includes an accessible summary of contemporary theories about sexuality in chapter 8, entitled "The couple's psychic development, sex, gender and sexualities" (Morgan, 2019, pp. 126–151). Sexual terminology is peppered throughout the book, as indicated in the index. Is this an implicit acceptance that sex is an intrinsic part of couple life, even when absent? In the ten pages devoted to sexual matters, Morgan considers some of the theories addressing the mysteries, conflicts and complexities of sex, including, for example, Glasser's (1979) core complex, which concerns the primitive claustro-agoraphobic nature of intimacy, and Target's assertion of the enigmatic and unknowable quality of sex. In particular Morgan focuses on the couple dynamics of loss of desire, which is a frequent presenting problem in psychotherapy, and the inevitable changes in sexual coupling and sensual play over the course of life. The overall impression is that sex continues to be seen as a stepping stone into the emotional world of the couple, which it is, but the physicality of sex seems to be explored with less ease and with less conviction. This observation begs the question, what does integration in the theory, training and practice of couple psychotherapy look like? Is it possible?

Separating sex and attachment

Since Freud's (1912) original formulation of psychic splitting, major psychoanalytic theorists have not progressed significantly towards integration. The erotic is mostly absent in Klein and Winnicott, who consider the mother-infant nursing couple as the prototype for the adult sexual couple, possibly stretching the credibility of their theories on sexuality. The formulations of both Freud and Bowlby suggest sex as something separate from adult affection, but infer interconnections one with the other (Clulow, 2009). Within Bowlby's (1988) attachment theory, sex is a distinct behavioural system separate from love, with its own motivational and functional systems, triggers and deactivating mechanisms (Mikulincer & Shaver, 2007). These four eminent psychoanalysts, Freud, Bowlby, Klein and Winnicott, are divided and this is the conundrum: did sex go out of psychoanalysis, only to be claimed by behaviourists preoccupied with performance because the sensuous co-existence of the mother-baby unit was not a credible platform for adult sexual relationships? Or are civilisation and instinctual life antagonistic, leaving human beings destined to split off their sexual desire, incapable of integrating love and sex, as Freud declares?

Drawing on Mitchell (2003) and Eagle (2007), Lichtenberg (2007) proposes that love, defined as attachment intimacy, and desire, defined as sexual lust, are inherently antagonistic, because loving attachment thrives on security, whereas desire thrives on novelty and diversity. Erotic desire is a powerful driver of initial coupling and then bonding, and for many people reduces over time (Mitchell, 2003). However, Eagle (2007, p. 43) suggests that when secure attachment is the prevailing drive for partners, they are likely to have chosen a mate who is "optimally similar", that is similar enough for the attachment bond to feel secure and safe, yet dissimilar enough to avoid triggering the incest taboo and inhibiting desire. Thus securely attached couples are more likely to maintain an active sexual life together. The prospects for couples who are insecurely attached are different: anxiously attached individuals tend to experience their partner as too similar to their early attachment figure, and become too clinging, killing off the other's desire. Avoidantly attached individuals may experience their partners as too different from early attached figures; sex then becomes detached from caring intimacy (Eagle, 2007). The influence of the two systems, attachment and sexuality, one on the other, is thought to be bidirectional. Nonetheless, the two biological systems are separate, implying that integration is challenging to all couples, and particularly so to those who are insecurely attached. The latter comprise the majority of the clinical population.

Be that as it may, the fact that in human beings the two systems of attachment and sexuality are separate does not explain the theoretical fragmentation of sex therapy since Masters and Johnson. The purely behavioural treatments created by this duo are perhaps evidence that, in terms of motivations, anxieties, defences and their impact on the adult couple, psychoanalysis went out of sex, just as sex went out of psychoanalysis. If there is an absence of the other in both paradigms, might that be because there has been a lack of theory linking the two? And what might underlie this lack? Is there perhaps something Oedipal about a couple therapist *either* working only with the sexual dimension *or* avoiding discussing sex altogether? Symbolically speaking, why might the psychodynamic couple psychotherapist stay outside the bedroom, avoiding any knowledge of the sexual encounter and focusing only about the emotional experience of the couple? Why might the sex therapist focus on the bed, seeing only two bodies attempting to interact or avoiding it, as if sex were primarily physical? Why is the (parental) bedroom door pivotal in couple treatment?

Challenging the profession

The challenges to practitioners of developing an integrated approach to mind, body and relationship in couple work are many and may begin with training. Senior psychotherapists who are qualified supervisors criticise current professional trainings which separate sexual behaviour and do not connect partners' responses to the tactile homework with the emotional-relational:

> I supervise a lot of psychosexual therapists, sex therapists who use sensate focus fairly routinely, and with whom I do battle about it. I haven't really sat down and had a think about why it is that my supervisees might not get it. They've learnt in a particular way that that's what they do.
>
> You need all your therapeutic skills and your eyes in order to use it [sensate focus] as part of the therapy, and I think some of the younger practitioners have it as a garden shed that's a stand-alone structure.

Separating sex from relationships is not limited to approved trainings: it permeates all aspects of professional practice. Consider first the couples who seek help. Generally clients find broaching sexual problems difficult and are afraid at least initially of disclosing sexual problems in the sessions. Their anxiety may be compounded by the inexperienced therapist's own fears, even though she has been trained in sexual topics:

> Actually talking through sexual experience in detail and what words you use and all those sorts of things, that's possibly shaming, very embarrassing and intrusive for both clients and therapists.
>
> It takes a lot of internal work on yourself to be able to understand where you're coming from and how difficult it is for you as an individual to talk in that specific way about sex.

Reflecting on the total transference operating in the clinical session is essential: a young therapist or student feeling anxious about discussing sex may be mirroring in her countertransference the client's lack of confidence:

> One of my supervisees working with a difficult couple doesn't feel very confident about taking their sexual problem up with them and so I'm thinking, "I know you've been trained because I've been part of that". A therapist has got to be able to go there. I think the issue is probably going to be that there's erectile dysfunction and a loss of confidence and that's been reflected by my supervisee feeling she's not confident to take this up.

Body, mind and relationship are indivisible in sexual matters, yet there is little integration of sex and sensate focus in couple psychotherapy. Is it possible that an innate anxiety around sex contaminates the profession? Just as sexuality and dependence are key issues for couples in therapy, so they may be problematic in the context of psychotherapy training and practice. Training institutions need to be capable of operating as a "secure-enough base" for practitioners, providing enough security to enable the work to be done competently, while generating a degree of insecurity to foster resilience and vitality in their members (Obholzer, 2001, p. 185). It appears that sexual anxieties travel through the psychotherapeutic community, that is trainers, therapists and clients. Using the metaphor of miners who contract silicosis from coal dust, Obholzer (2001, p. 189) proposes that the innate anxiety of the "raw material" of the work permeates psychotherapy organisations, and that inevitably the "psychic dust" of clients' distress is ingested by trainees. This contamination by couples' innate anxiety and psychic dust resonates with experienced psychotherapists who have identified a self-perpetuating cycle of training and practice that unconsciously maintains the professional status quo of non-integration of sex.

Against this backcloth, psychotherapists have to work out for themselves how to incorporate the senses, sensuality and sex into their practice and are using sensate focus *selectively* as an effective route to a more integrated approach in couple work. Of note, even highly experienced couple psychotherapists might find working in an integrated way a challenge. As one senior therapist said, "I prefer not to go into psychosexual work". There are myriad factors that might contribute to their feelings of unease, beginning with the very nature of sex. Human sexuality, as Freud discovered, is both a key organiser of psychological function and a deeply mysterious phenomenon. Since Freud, many eminent psychoanalysts have written about the madness of being in love and experiencing passionate desire, for example Orbach (2000) and Phillips (2006). According to Phillips, "sane sex" is a contradiction in terms, since "all our stories about the madness of love are stories of impossible conflict" (2006, p. 128). Moreover, sex is immensely complex (Fonagy, 2008), inherently dysregulated (Lemma, 2017) and defies being reduced to a theory (Clulow, 2009). From a psychoanalytic perspective, sexuality is a "zone of catastrophe": an individual's experience of himself is altered profoundly in sexual encounters, in that his desire begets desire and his excitement is mirrored in and mounts with the perceived experience of the other (Fonagy, 2009, p. xx). Crucially sex "involves the fragmentation of the self":

> As Fairbairn taught us, the splitting of self can become the convenient host for neurotic conflict.
>
> (Fonagy, 2009, p. xx)

Such comments may reflect the idea proposed by Winnicott (1960) that the individual's task of integration is never completely achieved and splitting to various degrees is unavoidable and universal. Clients' unconscious experiences of these processes are inevitably conveyed to therapists in the countertransference. Small wonder in this case that psychotherapists grapple with the task of integrating psychodynamic treatment approaches and sensate focus. Nonetheless, this intervention provides a useful tool to explore in the present and in appropriate detail their clients' shared experience of sensual-sexual contact. Perhaps then a *critical* difference between therapists working with both modalities and others who do not lays in their expectation that talking about sex, particularly the affective component of sexual relationships illuminated by the tactile exercises, will necessarily be part of couple work. As one integrated therapist said, "How you could see couples and not have the psychosexual add-on baffled me a bit". Psychotherapists need to acquire a particular professional skill: a well-developed "sexual interviewing skin", as Kahr (2009, pp. 7–8) describes the willingness to be curious and concerned about couples' sexual material without being excited or intrusive, all in the service of couple development. For integrated psychotherapists, the use of sensate focus helps maintain their competence and willingness to talk about sex.

Reviewing successful integrated approaches

A key question is this: are more and more couple psychotherapists in the western world now integrating sexual and psychic intercourse, as asserted for the UK by Boerma and Wrottesley (2020) and for the USA by Trusty-Smith (2020)? Are there successful integrated approaches explained in professional textbooks? Generally Helen Singer Kaplan's work is well regarded, as discussed earlier in this chapter. Interestingly she proposes working purely behaviourally with couples on sexual issues in the first instance, introducing psychodynamic interventions only when behavioural models proved ineffective. That said, Kaplan does not explain her theoretical concepts in depth; her manual (1987) assumes readers' psychoanalytical knowledge and skills in its application, possibly because she was addressing fellow psychiatrists of her era who were well trained in Freudian theory. Placing Kaplan aside, have other authors succeeded in integrating mind, body and relationship?

Reading Scharff and Savege Scharff

The most noteworthy examples of the interweaving of the unconscious relationship and sensate focus in couple psychotherapy are Scharff and Savege Scharff (1991, 2004), Scharff (1982, 2001), Caruso (2003, 2011, 2014a, 2014b) and Green and Seymour (2009). In their object relations approach to couple therapy, Scharff and Savege Scharff (1991) draw on psychoanalytical theories of Fairbairn (1952) and Klein (1946), in particular Klein's concept of projective identification, while their sex therapy model incorporates the behavioural tools of Masters and Johnson (1970) alongside the psychodynamic interventions proposed by Kaplan (1974, 1987). Drawing on the Winnicottian concept of the psychosomatic partnership, the earliest attachment relationship, to inform their use of sensate focus, Scharff and Savege Scharff (1991, p. 21) suggest that the intense shared physical experience of birth and then the infantile experience of the "intimate contact and arms-around holding" of the mother are evoked in the adult sexual partnership. The latter offers the only other experience of intense pleasure that is entirely somatic at the same time as it is entirely psychological.

Scharff and Savege Scharff (1991) provide a considered, detailed sequence of sex therapy exercises in a three-page diagrammatic table, describing the behavioural assignments of each phase and linking them to specific object relations issues and therapeutic goals. In the beginning of the sex therapy work, the co-authors prescribe the same non-erogenous touching to all couples, which brings up issues of basic trust, the partners' past experience of their mother's holding and of bodily integrity, for example. The aim at this stage, suggest the co-authors, is to allow the self to develop and *to be*, similar to the Winnicottian concept of the environment mother and her infant. The second phase of the exercises invites the couple to cooperate to maintain a holding environment together; the self is now in pleasurable interaction with the other. In reviews of the homework the therapist attends to the points at which couples experience difficulty: "Issues deeply buried are brought forcefully to the surface by the pressure of the physical interaction, by its successes and its failures" (Scharff & Savege Scharff, 1991, p. 189). The co-authors assert that the therapist then uses interpretation to understand the dynamics of the behavioural interaction:

> We are working on the mediation of internal object relations in the transition from infantile dependency to mature interdependency between two whole people who are involved in genital interaction. In the midphase of sex therapy, issues of the mediation of good and bad object relations can be seen in action during the artificially framed sexual interaction.
>
> (Scharff & Savege Scharff, 1991, p. 189)

The later phases of Scharff and Savege Scharff's programme contain many more behavioural tasks than mutual caressing: for example, genital self-examination and the 'squeeze' technique for premature ejaculation, each designed to a specific sexual dysfunction.

In terms of thinking about sensate focus and analysing couples' responses to it through a psychoanalytic lens, this book, *Object Relations Couple Therapy*, by Scharff and Savege Scharff (1991) is outstanding in its richness; it is convincing and thorough. No doubt because of these qualities, later authors, including Caruso (2011) and implicitly Green and Seymour (2009), have drawn on Scharff and Savege Scharff's thinking. Given that this book was published in 1991, it is remarkable that so few psychotherapists have attempted to advance and extend the authors' theories of the intervention. However, the two co-authors have continued to add to the discourse. In one paper, Scharff and Savege Scharff (2004) use a series of graded exercises, which the client couple seem to enjoy initially, but then they withdraw when the touching of breasts and genitals is introduced. The authors link the couple's 'stuck' position to one partner's psychosomatic symptom, the woman's sore throat, and a timely dream. They interpret this clinical material as manifestations of the couple's shared oral aggression and fear of it: "the exercises accelerated the emergence of anxiety located in the sex organs" (Scharff & Savege

Scharff, 2004, p. 475). An interesting impression from the Scharffs' writings is that they seem to separate couple therapy and sex therapy, regarding the latter as a separate contract to be discussed and agreed with the clients. Might this allude to a felt challenge of moving psychotherapeutically between mind, body and relationship? It was a challenge corroborated by my own study.

Reading Caruso

Caruso (2011) draws on Kaplan (1974), Scharff and Savege Scharff (1991) and Bowlby's (1988) attachment theory to explore imaginatively the unconscious relational aspects of a couple using sensate focus. The tasks, she claims, evoke behaviours and responses of attachment, including proximity-seeking behaviour, shared sensual activity and exploration of each other's body. Separations and reunions are experienced as couples start and end each exercise. Caruso claims that sensate focus has the potential to trigger preverbal experiences and evoke early mother-child experiences; couples may build trust and felt security as they share the early exercises and work through their anxieties. Progressing through the programme, partners are invited by the therapist to share greater sexual intimacy and cooperation, which for Caruso (2011, p. 121) are "features of relatedness". Exercises are selected to address specific sexual dysfunctions as well as the couple's unconscious internal working models and object relations. The author proposes that premature ejaculation, for example, is symptomatic of fear of engulfment and concern about the destructive power of the penis, leading to anxiety about arousal. She suggests that confusion between excitement and aggression in self and other might thus interfere with the individual's ability to allow his pleasurable bodily sensations. Such conflicts are then addressed verbally in the next therapy session, using transference and countertransference experiences, when the two partners report on their homework. Caruso then illustrates her integrated approach, which is both psychoanalytical and behavioural, skilfully using a complex case study published earlier in 2003.

Of particular relevance to the topic of this book, the author comments towards the end of her 2011 paper that her combined therapeutic model has the potential to confuse clients because of the conflicting goals and types of interventions associated with each paradigm. From subsequent correspondence with Caruso in 2023, however, it transpires that this comment was not in her original submission to the journal in question. It was the journal's reviewer who asked Caruso to add that mixing sex therapy with psychoanalytic techniques could be detrimental and confusing and the author modified her paper to allay the reviewer's concerns. In fact, from the start of her training Caruso learned how to work combining both approaches, which enables her to move comfortably between the two in clinical work.

Reading Green and Seymour

Like Caruso, Green and Seymour (2009) offer an illuminating, detailed case study that creatively integrates psychoanalytic and attachment theories with psychosexual therapy to address the couple's sexual problems. The authors consider the deeper disturbances of the presenting symptom, loss of desire. They provide a clear overview of the progress of the therapy, as the partners explore themselves and their relationship and work through their developmental challenges. The design of the chapter uses three different but interwoven typographical styles to distinguish between firstly, the couple's narrative; secondly, the therapists' psychodynamic and psychosexual interventions, which are behavioural, biomedical and educational; and thirdly, the rationale behind the selected interventions. Sensate focus is one of the tools used. Green and Seymour (2009, p. 151) propose that its specific purpose in this case study is to "bring anxiety down to manageable levels", and to modify *spectatoring*. The latter is a term devised by Masters and Johnson (1970) to describe a person's sense of detachment during sexual encounters, often watching his own body and genitals rather than feeling engaged in the arousal process. The authors also use the tactile intervention to enhance sensuality and improve self-knowledge and communication between the partners; they suggest that in addition, the homework helps raise and resolve issues of trust: both the couple's trust in the therapist and trust between the partners. During the sensate focus programme, the couple's gradual development goes hand in hand with the emergence of their anxieties and defences: the yearning for magical symbiosis, connecting with and fearing vulnerability and neediness, fears of destructiveness and aggression, having a safe haven, managing a rush of primitive feelings, separation anxieties, fears of disintegration, Oedipal anxieties, unconscious fears of castration, loss, mourning and ambivalence.

Green and Seymour's (2009) chapter is convincingly written. The missing link in this thorough and insightful case description is perhaps the detailed references of the theories applied, informing the couple work as it focuses on both psyche and soma; and where the therapists' clinical observations confirm or depart from the theories. A bibliography would have been a valuable addition for teaching purposes, if integrated approaches are to be developed bidirectionally, that is, within both psychodynamic couple psychotherapy training and psychosexual therapy training.

Summarising the context

In summary, in the 21st century there is some evidence of professional efforts to integrate psychoanalytic (including psychodynamic) and psychosexual approaches in the treatment of couples with sexual problems. However, the splitting of psyche and soma remains rife, though not universal, within the profession as well as the clinical population. There are three critical, parallel developments in our field that illuminate the continuing phenomenon of splitting today. These are, firstly, the changing relationship of psychoanalysis and sex over the decades; secondly, the evolution of couple psychotherapy in the UK; and thirdly, the creation of sensate focus as a core tool in the behavioural sex therapy designed by Masters and Johnson (1970). The fact that few texts exist that describe credible, successful theoretical and clinical integration of body, mind and relationship in couple work highlights the professional challenge of working with sexual relationships.

References

Balfour, A. (1993–2021) 'A brief history of Tavistock Relationships', in Waddell, M. and Kraemer, S. (eds.) *The Tavistock century. 2020 vision.* Bicester: Phoenix Publishing House.

Balint, E. (1968) 'Unconscious communications between husband and wife', in Ruszczynski, S. (ed.) *Psychotherapy with couples. Theory and practice at the Tavistock Institute of Marital Studies.* London: Karnac, pp. 30–43.

Bannister, K., Garden, V., Hall, J., Lyons, A., Phillipson, H., Pincus, L., Seligman, E. and Stephens, J. (1960) *Marriage: Studies in emotional conflict and growth.* London: Tavistock Institute of Human Relations.

Bannister, K., Lyons, A., Pincus, L., Robb, J., Shooter, A. and Stephens, J. (1955) *Social casework in marital problems. The development of a psychodynamic approach.* London: Tavistock Publications.

Bannister, K. and Pincus, L. (1965) *Shared phantasy in marital problems: Therapy in a four-person relationship.* London: Family Discussion Bureau and Tavistock Institute of Human Relations.

Berry, M.D. (2013) 'The history and evolution of sex therapy and its relationship to psychoanalysis', *International Journal of Applied Psychoanalytic Studies*, 10(1), pp. 53–74. https://doi.org/10.1002/aps.1315

Berry, M.D. (2014) *Towards a psychodynamically-informed model for the integrative psychotherapeutic treatment of male sexual dysfunction.* PhD thesis, University College London [Online]. http://ethos.bl.uk (Accessed: 3 February 2016).

Bion, W.R. (1962) *Learning from experience.* London: Tavistock.

Boerma, M. and Wrottesley, C. (2020) 'Two responses to "Should 'sensate focus' have a place in couple psychoanalytic psychotherapy?" The development of integrated training at Tavistock Relationships', *Couple and Family Psychoanalysis*, 10(2), pp. 198–202.

Bowlby, J. (1988) *A secure base. Clinical applications of attachment theory.* London: Routledge.

Britton, R. (1989) 'The missing link: Parental sexuality in the Oedipus complex', in Steiner, J. (ed.) *The Oedipus complex today.* London: Karnac, pp. 83–102.

Carpy, D.V. (1989) 'Tolerating the countertransference: A mutative process', *International Journal of Psychoanalysis*, 70, pp. 287–294.

Caruso, N. (2003) 'Object relations theory and technique applied to sex and marital therapy', *Journal of Applied Psychoanalytic Studies*, 5(3), pp. 297–308.

Caruso, N. (2011) 'The entangled nature of attachment and sexuality in the couple relationship', *Couple and Family Psychoanalysis*, 1(1), pp. 117–135.

Caruso, N. (2014a) 'Addressing sexual issues in couple psychotherapy', in Scharff, D.E. and Savege Scharff, J. (eds.) *Psychoanalytic couple therapy.* London: Karnac, pp. 237–245.

Caruso, N.J. (2014b) 'Sexual desire disorder: A case study from a dynamic perspective', *Couple and Family Psychoanalysis*, 4(2), pp. 166–185.

Clulow, C. (ed.). (2001) *Adult attachment and couple psychotherapy.* London: Brunner Routledge.

Clulow, C. (2009) 'The facts of life: An introduction', in Clulow, C. (ed.) *Sex, attachment and couple psychotherapy*. London: Karnac, pp. xxv–xli.

Clulow, C. and Boerma, M. (2009) 'Dynamics and disorders of sexual desire', in Clulow, C. (ed.) *Sex, attachment and couple psychotherapy*. London: Karnac, pp. 75–101.

Clulow, C., Hertzmann, L. and Nyberg, V. (2018) 'Couple psychoanalysis in the United Kingdom: Past, present and future', *Psychoanalytic Inquiry*, 38(5), pp. 364–377. 10.1080/07351690.2018.1469901

Colman, W. (2009) 'What do we mean by "sex"?', in Clulow, C. (ed.) *Sex, attachment and couple psychotherapy*. London: Karnac, pp. 25–44.

DeRogatis, L.R. (2007) 'A response to Rowland's, "Will medical solutions to sexual problems make sexological care and science obsolete?"', *Journal of Sex & Marital Therapy*, 33(5), pp. 421–425.

Deutsch, F. (1957) 'A footnote to Freud's "Fragment of an analysis of a case of hysteria"', *Psychoanalytic Quarterly*, 26, pp. 159–167.

Dicks, H.V. (1967) *Marital tensions*. London: Routledge & Kegan Paul.

Eagle, M. (2007) 'Attachment and sexuality', in Diamond, D., Blatt, S.J. and Lichtenberg, J.D. (eds.) *Attachment and sexuality*. New York: The Analytic Press, pp. 269.

Ellis, H.H. (1897–1928) *Psychology of sex. A manual for students*. 2nd edn. New York: Harcourt, 1978.

Fairbairn, W.R.D. (1952) *Psychoanalytic studies of the personality*. Hove: Tavistock Publications, Routledge and Kegan Paul.

Fisher, J.V. (1999) *The uninvited guest. Emerging from narcissism towards marriage*. London: Karnac Books.

Fonagy, P. (2008) 'A genuinely developmental theory of sexual enjoyment and its implications for psychoanalytic technique', *Journal of the American Psychoanalytic Association*, 56(1), pp. 11–36.

Fonagy, P. (2009) 'Foreword', in Clulow, C. (ed.) *Sex, attachment and couple psychotherapy*. London: Karnac, pp. xvii–xxiii.

Freud, S. (1905) 'Three essays on sexuality and other works', in *Standard edition 7*. London: The Hogarth Press, pp. 123–246.

Freud, S. (1910) 'The future prospects of psychoanalytic therapy', in *Standard edition 19*. London: The Hogarth Press, pp. 139–152.

Freud, S. (1912) 'On the universal tendency to debasement in the sphere of love (Contributions to the psychology of love II)', in *Standard edition 11*. London: The Hogarth Press and the Institute of Psychoanalysis, pp. 177–190.

Freud, S. (1917) 'Introductory lectures on psychoanalysis', in *Standard edition 16*. London: The Hogarth Press, 1961.

Freud, S. (1923) 'The ego and the id', in *Standard edition 19*. London: The Hogarth Press, 1923–1925, pp. 1–66.

Glasser, M. (1979) 'Some aspects of the role of aggression in the perversions', in Rosen, I. (ed.) *Sexual deviation*. 2nd edn. Oxford: Oxford University Press, pp. 278–305.

Goodwach, R. (2005) 'Sex therapy: Historical evolution, current practice. Part 1', *Australian and New Zealand Journal of Family Therapy*, 26(3), pp. 155–164.

Green, L. and Seymour, J. (2009) 'Loss of desire: A psychosexual case study', in Clulow, C. (ed.) *Sex, attachment and couple psychotherapy*. London: Karnac, pp. 141–163.

Grier, F. (2001–2005) 'No sex couples, catastrophic change and the primal scene', in Grier, F. (ed.) *Oedipus and the couple*. London: Karnac, pp. 201–219.

Heimann, P. (1950) 'On countertransference', *International Journal of Psychoanalysis*, 31, pp. 81–84.

Joseph, B. (1985) 'Transference: the total situation', *International Journal of Psychoanalysis*, 66(4), pp. 457–464.

Kahr, B. (2009) 'Psychoanalysis and sexpertise', in Clulow, C. (ed.) *Sex, attachment and couple psychotherapy*. London: Karnac, pp. 1–23.

Kahr, B. (2012) 'Foreword', in Balfour, A., Morgan, M. and Vincent, C. (eds.) *How couple relationships shape our world. Clinical practice, research and policy perspectives*. London: Karnac, pp. xvii–xxii.

Kaplan, H.S. (1974) *The new sex therapy*. New York: Times Books.

Kaplan, H.S. (1987) *The illustrated manual of sex therapy*. 2nd edn. New York: Brunner Mazel.

Kaplan, H.S. (1995) *The sexual desire disorders. Dysfunctional regulation of sexual motivation*. New York: Brunner/Mazel.

Kinsey, A.C., Pomeroy, W.B., Martin, C.E. and Gebhard, P. (1948) *Sexual behavior in the human male*. Philadelphia: W.B. Saunders.

Kinsey, A.C., Pomeroy, W.B., Martin, C.E. and Gebhard, P. (1953) *Sexual behavior in the human female*. Philadelphia: W.B. Saunders.

Klein, M. (1946) 'Notes on some schizoid mechanisms', *International Journal of Psychoanalysis*, 27, pp. 99–110.

Kolodny, R.C. (1981) 'Evaluating sex therapy: Process and outcome at the Masters & Johnson Institute', *The Journal of Sex Research*, 17(4), pp. 301–318. https://doi.org/10.1080/00224498109551123

Laplanche, J. and Pontalis, J.B. (1983) *The language of psychoanalysis*. London: The Hogarth Press.

Lemma, A. (2017) 'The sex worker as mirror: Distinguishing affirming from defensive use of sex workers', in *Psychosexual conference 2017. Body image and the sexual self: How anxieties about our bodies affect sexual relationships*, London: Tavistock Relationships.

Lichtenberg, J. (2007) 'A discussion of eight essays', in Diamond, D., Blatt, S.J. and Lichtenberg, J. (eds.) *Attachment and sexuality*. New York: The Analytic Press, pp. 237–261.

LoPiccolo, J. (1994) 'The evolution of sex therapy', *Sexual and Marital Therapy*, 9(1), pp. 5–7. https://doi.org/10.1080/02674659408409562

Masters, W.H. and Johnson, V.E. (1966) *Human sexual response*. Boston: Little, Brown & Co.

Masters, W.H. and Johnson, V.E. (1970) *Human sexual inadequacy*. Boston: Little, Brown & Co.

Mattinson, J. and Sinclair, I. (1979) *Mate and stalemate*. London: Institute of Marital Studies 1981.

McCabe, M., Althof, S.E., Assalian, P., Chevret-Measson, M., Leiblum, S.R., Simonelli, C. and Wylie, K. (2010) 'Psychological and interpersonal dimensions of sexual function and dysfunction', *Journal of Sexual Medicine*, 7, pp. 327–336.

Mikulincer, M. and Shaver, P.R. (2007) 'A behavioral systems perspective of the psychodynamics of attachment and sexuality', in Diamond, D., Blatt, S.J. & Lichtenberg, J. (eds.) *Attachment and sexuality*. New York: The Analytic Press, pp. 51–78.

Mitchell, S.A. (2003) *Can love last? The fate of romance over time*. New York: W W Norton.

Morgan, M. (2019) *A couple state of mind. Psychoanalysis of couples and the Tavistock Relationships model*. Abingdon: Routledge.

Obholzer, A. (2001) 'Security and creativity at work', in Clulow, C. (ed.) *Adult attachment and couple psychotherapy*. London: Brunner-Routledge, pp. 185–193.

Orbach, S. (2000) *The impossibility of sex*. Harmondsworth: Penguin.

Phillips, A. (2006) *Going sane*. London: Faber and Faber.

Rowland, D.L. (2007) 'Will medical solutions to sexual problems make sexological care and science obsolete?', *Journal of Sex & Marital Therapy*, 33(5), pp. 385–397.

Ruszczynski, S. (1993a) 'Thinking about and working with couples', in Ruszczynski, S. (ed.) *Psychotherapy with couples. Theory and practice at the Tavistock Institute of Marital Studies*. London: Karnac, pp. 197–217.

Ruszczynski, S. (1993b) 'The theory and practice of the Tavistock Institute of Marital Studies', in Ruszczynski, S. (ed.) *Psychotherapy with couples. Theory and practice at the Tavistock Institute of Marital Studies*. London: Karnac, pp. 3–23.

Ruszczynski, S. (1995) 'Narcissistic object relating', in Ruszczynski, S. and Fisher, J. (eds.) *Intrusiveness and intimacy in the couple*. London: Karnac, pp. 13–32.

Ruszczynski, S.P. (1992) 'Notes towards a psychoanalytic understanding of the couple relationship', *Psychoanalytic Psychotherapy*, 6(1), pp. 33–48.

Saxon, W. (1995) 'Dr. Helen Kaplan, 66, dies; Pioneer in sex therapy field', *The New York Times*, 19 August (Accessed: 27 May 2013). https://www.nytimes.com/1995/08/19/obituaries/dr-helen-kaplan-66-dies-pioneer-in-sex-therapy-field.html

Scharff, D.E. (1982) *The sexual relationship. An object relations view of sex and the family*. Boston: Routledge and Kegan Paul.

Scharff, D.E. (2001) 'Applying psychoanalysis to couple psychotherapy: The treatment of a couple with sexualised persecutory internal objects resulting from trauma', *Journal of Applied Psychoanalytic Studies*, 3(4), pp. 325–351.

Scharff, D.E. and Savege Scharff, J. (1991) *Object relations couple therapy*. London: Jason Aronson.

Scharff, D.E. and Savege Scharff, J. (2004) 'Using dreams in treating couples' sexual issues', *Psychoanalytic Inquiry*, 24(3), pp. 468–482.

Sheldon, M. (2008) 'The man who discovered sex', *Telegraph Magazine*, 5 March, pp. 22–26.

Sutherland, J.D. (1954) 'Introduction', *Social casework in marital problems. The development of a psychodynamic approach*. London: Tavistock Publications 1955, pp. ix–xii.

Tiefer, L. (2006) 'Sex therapy as a humanistic enterprise', *Sexual and Relationship Therapy*, 21(3), pp. 359–379.

Trusty-Smith, C. (2020) 'Commentary on integrative teaching and treatment modalities in couple psychosexual therapy: Reply to Susan Pacey', *Couple and Family Psychoanalysis*, 10(2), pp. 203–207.

von Krafft-Ebing, R. (1886) *Psychopathia sexualis*. (Translated by Chaddock, C.G). 7th edn. Philadelphia: The F. A. Davis Co., 1893.

Waldinger, M.D. (2007) 'Revival of medical sexology in psychiatry of the 21st century', *Primary Psychiatry*, 14(2), pp. 35–36.

Waldinger, M.D. (2008) 'Letter to the Editor. Not medical solutions, but overmedicalization by pharmaceutical company policies endanger both sexological care, science and sexual medicine. A commentary', *Journal of Sex & Marital Therapy*, 34(3), pp. 179–183.

Waldinger, M.D. (2015) 'Sexual dysfunctions: What can be done?', *European Psychiatry*, 30, pp. 28–31.

Winnicott, D.W. (1960) 'The theory of the parent-infant relationship', *International Journal of Psychoanalysis*, 41, pp. 585–595.

Chapter 3

Sensing

Conceiving the tactile programme as technique

Sensate focus was created originally by Masters and Johnson (1970) to address marital sexual problems through sensual-sexual behaviour and feedback, deliberately bypassing emotional-relational patterns that might lie beneath patients' sexual distress. Although the duo's separating of body from mind and relationship was a flawed approach, a reflective, skilled therapist needs to start with detailed knowledge of the phases and behavioural steps, if she seeks to integrate sensate focus into couple work in a creative, developmental way. This chapter therefore covers past and current prescriptions of the tactile intervention. Thereafter theories of the body as a repository of unconscious experience are summarised, along with highlights of new research on the neurobiology of the senses and its implications for the tactile intervention in couple therapy.

Sensate focus, a cognitive-behavioural programme of mutual touching and caressing exercises for couples to do at home, has been the cornerstone of psychosexual therapy since the 1970s (Linschoten et al., 2016). Although there are three earlier treatises on 'sensate' techniques, the first written by John Hunter (1786), the second more advanced model by Joseph Wolpe (1958), and the third by Arnold A. Lazarus (1965), it was Masters and Johnson (1970) who developed and named sensate focus in their landmark book, *Human Sexual Inadequacy*, following their 11-year study of human sexual disorders. Having devised the first brief, intensive therapy programme for couples presenting with sexual problems, Masters and Johnson claimed a treatment success rate of 75–80%, which was considered "impressive and enormously encouraging" (Belliveau & Richter, 1970, p. 3). Their research and techniques were groundbreaking and became highly influential in the field of sexuality, displacing psychoanalysis as the primary treatment model, and launching sex therapy as a discipline in its own right (LoPiccolo, 1994; Berry, 2013). Their approach to sexual fulfilment, however, was later criticised for being too focused on physical performance with little regard for the emotional and psychological side of relationships (*The Daily Telegraph*, 2013, p. 27). Did they know about partners' vast wealth of unsymbolised experience stored in the body and mobilised by touch? By separating body from mind in the treatment of sexual

DOI: 10.4324/9781003328292-3

difficulties, this pioneering couple were in effect attempting to divide the indivisible, a state of play that arguably has been slow to change in the field of couple psychotherapy.

Clarifying the concept of sensate focus

The centrepiece of Masters and Johnson's work, sensate focus is defined today as:

> a hierarchy of invariant, structured touching and discovery suggestions ... and ... a diagnostic and therapeutic tool for identifying psychological and relationship factors that contribute to sexual difficulties, and for teaching new skills to overcome these problems and to foster more meaningful sexual intimacy.
>
> (Weiner & Avery-Clark, 2014, p. 308)

Three years later, Weiner and Avery-Clark (2017, p. 8) offer a further, reconsidered definition:

> a series of structured and discovery suggestions that provides opportunities for experiencing your own and your partner's bodies in a non-demand, exploratory way without having to read each other's minds. Non-demand exploration is defined as touching for your own interest without regard for trying to make sexual response, pleasure, enjoyment or relaxation happen for yourself or your partner, or prevent them from happening. Touching for your own interest is further defined as focusing on the touch sensations of temperature, pressure, and texture. Temperature, pressure, and texture are even more specifically defined as cool or warm, hard or soft (firm or light), and smooth or rough.

The following details of the intervention are based on six significant sources: the 'translation' of Masters and Johnson's techniques by Belliveau and Richter (1970), updates by Weiner and Avery-Clark (2014, 2017), Hawton's (1993) classical sex therapy guidelines, the systemic approach of Weeks et al. (2016), my study and my own extensive clinical experience. Appendix 1 offers a synthesis of these key sources. Critical differences are discussed in the main text of this chapter.

Starting phase 1 and moving to phase 2

Couples are invited to begin by preparing the room of their choice, which may or may not be their bedroom, making it warm and comfortable. They might then take a bath or shower, alone or together, to help them make the transition from the outside world to their couple space. In the *first phase*, regardless of type of sexual problem, the couple focus on their sensuality, exploring their own sensory experiences in turn while naked together and in the complete privacy of their own room, avoiding times of tiredness and stress. Couples are asked to agree in advance that no breasts, buttocks or genitals are touched at this stage and that erotic stimulation and intercourse are out of bounds. Couples may protest at this request and the therapist then explains that the rationale behind it is to avoid feelings of pressure to perform and to have a shared sense of safety. The latter facilitates relaxation.

First, one partner caresses the other, stroking the other's body from top to toe, so that both know what to expect, with no surprises. Each spouse stays focused on his or her own sensations and responses. The partners then change roles. They make note of their experiences of texture (warm, cold, smooth, rough) and of all the senses – whether positive, negative or neutral – and discuss them with the therapist in the following session. If couples report that they lost interest or concentration, or became bored, the therapist asks when and where they noticed the loss and what was happening at that moment.

Ideally in modern practice couples would do this exercise two or three times a week. The next phase or step is not introduced until the couple succeeds at the current one. In this first phase, the therapist aims to help partners minimise "spectatoring", a dissociative state, triggered by performance anxiety and fear of sexual failure, in which the individual is distracted from sexual stimuli because, for example, he is focusing anxiously on the strength of his erection (Masters & Johnson, 1970, p. 11). The important first phase is intended to be an experience in itself, which is neither a prelude to sex nor a form of foreplay.

Still in the *first phase*, touching now includes exploration of breasts and genitals without deliberate stimulation. Both partners continue to develop their awareness of their own physical sensations and avoid thinking about expectations of achieving a particular sexual response, either their own or their partner's. Neither partner assumes responsibility for the couple's sensuous responses. The couple are asked to make no effort to reach ejaculation or orgasm. However, some experience of pleasure is a good result. Sexual intercourse remains off limits. The *second phase* of the treatment is designed to address a particular sexual problem, such as erectile disorder or genito-pelvic pain and penetration disorder, and so other physiological interventions may be included. The couple may move gradually over many sessions to mutual masturbation, partial penetration and containment (penetration, if desired, without thrusting), and then finally thrusting to orgasm.

At this juncture, for couple psychotherapists working in an integrated way, I suggest *a crucial point of departure* from Weiner and Avery-Clark's guidelines (2017, p. 17). These two authors propose that therapists instruct clients to disallow anxiety by focusing on their own sensations, putting aside their feelings or emotions, especially anxiety. By contrast, the approach proposed in this book uses sensate focus *precisely* to mobilise emotional-relational anxieties and defences in each partner, so that these may thought about, discussed and worked through during therapy. Such anxieties are thus minimised and soothed. Within this integrated approach sensate focus becomes instrumental in the development of the partners as a creative couple (Morgan, 2019), more able to use their relationship to resolve sexual difficulties. An important point here is that in the early stages of therapy partners may be too defended or overwhelmed by anxiety to be able to carry out any tactile task together, and the timing of introducing sensate focus into the therapy has to be considered carefully, taking the couple's state of mind into account, as explained in the chapters that follow.

Correcting the confusion over goals and implementation

Confusion about Masters and Johnson's (1970) conceptualisation and implementation of their most famous treatment developed rapidly after the publication of *Human Sexual Inadequacy*. Controversy over its underlying message that sex was 'natural' was also widespread. According to Weiner and Avery-Clark (2017), who are both graduates of and formerly clinical staff at the Masters and Johnson Institute (MJI), Florida, USA, the goals of sensate focus and instructions on its use were poorly communicated initially. So much so that a 'translation' of Masters and Johnson's text into plain language was written and published in the same year as the original text (Belliveau & Richter, 1970).

As the founders' clinical experience grew over the years, the design of the intervention evolved significantly, and at their 25th anniversary event, Masters and Johnson made two major amendments to the *initial phase* of the exercises. These changes were incorporated into MJI's training materials in the 1980s (Kolodny, 1981), but failed to be disseminated beyond the comparatively few professionals who attended conferences or were involved in training and clinical work at the Institute (Weiner & Avery-Clark, 2014). These little-known amendments are of particular import to this book; they are first that each partner in turn aims simply to *touch*, thereby discounting an earlier principle of *pleasuring the other person*; the second change was that the touching partner is invited to focus on *his or her own sensations of touch* and *not* the sensations or pleasure of the touched partner. The revised aim now encourages each individual to become absorbed in his or her own sensory experience, developing an attitude of touching for his or her own interest (Weiner & Avery-Clark, 2017). The first phase is intended to be *an experience in itself, for the self* in the presence of the partner.

Today the misunderstanding that the early assignment is aimed at pleasing and pleasuring the spouse is widespread, whereas the objective is to focus on the client's own experience of touching and being in the tactile experience (Linschoten et al., 2016). Interestingly, Helen Singer Kaplan (1987, p. 27) made the error described earlier, making pleasuring the aim of the first phase of treatment, and did not amend her approach. In addition, the confusion over the goal and nature of the first phase of the prescribed exercises may have contributed to the proliferation of alternative prescriptions by practitioners. Therapists of various theoretical orientations have modified the intervention; for example, Schnarch (1997) and Zeitner (2013). There may be as many versions of sensate focus in the world as there are therapists using it.

Confirming the rationale and techniques underpinning the first phase

The first phase of sensate focus is often the most challenging and most rewarding phase for couples (Scharff & Savege Scharff, 1991). If, however, the fundamental skills of self-awareness at a sensory level are not learned, then a successful outcome of the exercise programme is unlikely (Weiner & Avery-Clark, 2017). The important, initial goal is for partners to minimise untenable, felt pressure to have sex or respond sexually in a particular way. Masters and Johnson's research in the 1960s demonstrated paradoxically that redirecting partners' attention onto sensory experience moment by moment through voluntary behaviour such as caressing allowed sexual feelings and physical responses to occur naturally. According to Weiner and Avery-Clark (2014, p. 310), "the sensory level of experience is the gateway to [the couple's] long-term goals of sexual arousal, pleasure and intimacy". Masters and Johnson were aware that the physiological and emotional sexual responses – for example, desire, arousal and orgasm – are not under voluntary control: an individual cannot force these responses at will. Sexual response is controlled by the autonomic nervous system and is a natural function of anatomy, biochemistry, physiology and other processes, the functioning of which can be altered negatively by anxiety and stress (Bancroft, 2008; Linschoten et al., 2016).

Nonetheless, the claim that sex was a natural function led to the claim by professional critics that Masters and Johnson were in denial of the impact of psychosocial phenomena on sexual response (Tiefer, 1995; Iasenza, 2001). A rebuttal of these criticisms by Weiner and Avery-Clark (2017) is that firstly, sexual response is a natural process in the same way that breathing, sleeping and emotions are natural processes that are not under an individual's immediate control; and secondly, that the celebrated couple fully acknowledged the psychosocial aspects of sexuality.

A further criticism of sensate focus is that it ignores the importance of couple psychodynamics in both cause and cure of sexual dysfunction and dissatisfaction (Levine, 2009). Although Masters and Johnson were well aware of the emotional-relational component of sexual functioning, they chose not to work with the affective dimension of couple relationships, and held the view that within their short (two-week) treatment model, countertransference issues, for example, would not arise (Belliveau & Richter, 1970; Masters & Johnson, 1970). Moreover, they claimed that touch was an essential means of human communication, giving "meaning to sexual responsiveness for both men and women" and potentially conveying "tenderness, affection, solace, understanding, desire, warmth, comfort" to their patients (Belliveau & Richter, 1970, p. 73).

Comparing the original setting and the current therapeutic frame

Masters and Johnson originally conceived sensate focus as the primary intervention in a residential, two-week Rapid Therapy Programme for couples. These exercises were conducted twice daily by couples in their private room and were supported by co-therapy verbal sessions, sexual education and group discussions, all taking place at the Reproductive Biology Research Foundation (RBRF) in St Louis (Belliveau & Richter, 1970). Belliveau and Richter (1970, p. 73) state clearly that "the relationship between the partners is the patient," an approach that is in common with couple psychotherapy in the 21st century (Morgan, 2019). Yet, as previously described, the relationship was assessed only in terms of partners' conscious communication of their physical responses to each other.

The brevity and intensity of the therapy offered by the RBRF, however, were a far cry from current practice in couple psychotherapy and psychosexual therapy in the UK. At Tavistock Relationships (TR), for example, the working frame is a weekly session of an hour. This begs the question as to *how* and *if* the therapeutic effectiveness of the tactile intervention in contemporary practice has been limited by the marked differences in therapeutic setting and frame. This concern appears not to have materialised: a critical literature review in 2016 found that sensate focus was generally supported "as a validated and effective sex therapy procedure" (Linschoten et al., 2016, p. 235). Decades after its launch, the intervention continues to be used by a large majority of practitioners in the field of sex therapy (Berry, 2014).

Broadening the original patient population

The RBRF's patient population on the residential programme was almost exclusively white, middle class, financially stable, able-bodied, heterosexual, married couples (Belliveau & Richter, 1970). Today in the UK and USA, therapists working in the field of sexology have developed the tactile exercises so that they can be used to treat a wide variety of clinical populations including but by no means limited to heterosexual, middle class couples (Linschoten et al., 2016).

Reviewing Hawton's classical guidelines

A key textbook that elaborates extensively on the principles and practice of sensate focus within classical sex therapy is Keith Hawton's (1993) *Sex Therapy: A Practical Guide*. This manual continues to be used widely in professional psychosexual therapy trainings. While highly prescriptive, Hawton sets out clearly and thoughtfully the parameters of the behavioural tasks for couples in treatment. The section on sensate focus (Hawton, 1993, pp. 121–140) provides a solid foundation in the details and application of this tool. Dividing the programme into two phases, "non-genital sensate focus" and "genital sensate focus", the author begins by proposing ways of introducing the step-by-step programme, and suggesting information to impart to clients, such as how long it will take overall, instructions for the first homework session, avoidance of intercourse, touching of breasts and genitals, and so forth. Hawton (1993) also advises the therapist how to respond to possible protests from the couple, how to guide the partners in negotiating homework appointments with each other and how often the exercises should be done. All these are carried out in the aim of creating a "relaxed approach to sexuality which . . . is sometimes sufficient to eliminate the presenting problem" (p. 128). The author advocates that partners rebuild their sexual relationship by learning to enjoy general physical contact first, which is the initial phase of the programme. The author's advice is that couples need to have had several enjoyable sessions and to have learned how to talk comfortably about sex before progressing to "genital sensate focus" (p. 133). During this, the second phase, states Hawton, couples are encouraged to try to stay with pleasurable feelings, although in some cases general disharmony and resentment may prevent the possibility of partners enjoying any physical interaction. Whether couples' reactions are positive, negative or something else, they are important material for processing in the next therapy session.

Noting Weeks, Gambescia and Hertlein's systemic approach

Systemic psychotherapists Weeks et al. (2016, p. 157) devote a whole chapter of their sex therapy manual to sensate focus and its application. In their minds, this behavioural intervention is designed to break the cycle of avoidance, or "negative reinforcement", in a relationship. The tactile exercises, these authors assert, are much more challenging than they might seem initially, not only to the therapist in designing an appropriate first step for the couple, but also to the couple who are anxious about physical intimacy. The authors advise that Kaplan's (1987) steps might be too ambitious for many couples who are then set up for failure. Starting slowly, by holding hands for example, with minute increments in the tasks, is paramount. Along with Brooks (1994), Weeks et al. (2016) are unusual in identifying the important, early goal of the tactile exercises in developing self-awareness in the presence of another and in gradually enabling the couple to connect with their own sensual feelings.

The chapter on sensate focus by Weeks et al. (2016) is illuminating and comprehensive in its coverage. However, the authors make no clear connection in the case examples between couples' responses to the exercises and the emotional-relational aspects of the presenting sexual problem, nor do they appear to consider the dynamics operating between therapist and the couple triggered by the introduction of the homework into the therapy.

Understanding touch as a gateway to the embodied unconscious

Generally sensate focus is poorly understood within the profession of psychotherapy, mostly because it is viewed, as described at the start of this chapter, as a concrete intervention teaching conscious sexual technique, and not as a gateway to the unconscious. By contrast, experienced psychotherapists who use this intervention in an integrated way view sexual relationships through a psychoanalytical lens and think about couples' unconscious dynamics mobilised by the caressing exercises.

For these therapists the most important function of the tactile intervention is its role in facilitating couple development, which is the principal goal of couple psychotherapy. They view the body as a repository of unconscious material and know that tactile exercises may help partners conceptualise unconscious embodied experience, thereby bringing it into their consciousness. Importantly therapists use the intervention to engage with the infant in the couple, explore past trauma, move away from dysfunctional early life learning and facilitate healthier, mature relating as adults. If the intervention is used in this way, the exercises have the potential to contribute to the couple's creation of a holding environment at home. These thoughts all resonate strongly with Winnicottian theory, as discussed subsequently.

Theorising the body as a repository of unconscious experience

Integrated psychotherapists use sensate focus and the body to gain access to couples' unconscious affective experience. The belief that the body is a repository of unconscious material is supported by psychoanalytical theory from Freud onwards. According to Freud (1900–1901), all experience moment to moment from the very beginning of life leaves a memory trace, which can never be lost, even if it is unavailable to conscious recall. In his concept of the "experiential conglomerate", derived from Freud, Winnicott (1968, p. 18) links a mother's own unconscious memory of being a baby to her "primary maternal preoccupation" and her competence, or otherwise, as a caregiver. The experiential conglomerate is a universal phenomenon:

> everyone has been a child. In each adult observer there is the whole memory of his infancy and childhood, both the fantasy and reality, in so far as it was appreciated at the time. Much is forgotten but nothing is lost. What better example could direct attention to the vast resources of the unconscious!
>
> (Winnicott, 1964, p. 147)

The key point here is that psychotherapists using the tactile intervention *think* psychoanalytically about their clients' responses to the exercises, but choose *not to work exclusively psychoanalytically* in the traditional sense. The hallmark of classical psychoanalysis is the therapist's interpretation of transference phenomena emerging from the client's unconscious. Interpretation can take many forms and whilst it is not purely a cerebral intervention, it is mostly a *top-down* approach, in the sense that it is a product of cortical processing by the analyst using language and symbolism to decode and interpret experience. Therapists can sense in their bodies the client's unconscious response, which is converted into something that can be symbolised and talked about. It is important to note, however, that some of the analyst's *behavioural* interventions can be overlooked when considering analytic technique. These interventions are fundamental to psychoanalytic work. They may or may not involve the analyst's voice or words: for example, setting and maintaining the frame, setting the fee, announcing the end of the session, the analyst's laughter and innumerable unconscious acts. All these are experiences that have unconscious meaning and contribute to the analytic process. Traditionally psychoanalysts have regarded or rejected sensate focus as a *non-analytic, bottom-up* technique, in the sense that it seeks to create a different kind of bodily experience to effect change. Therapists clearly use the tactile exercises in order to give couples a corrective experience that does not rely on language; their use of the homework debatably constitutes "interpretive action" (Ogden, 1994, p. 220). Their conscious intentions and thoughts (*top-down*) are to tap into couples' internal worlds through the body (*bottom-up*), helping each partner move nonverbal infantile experience into the verbal realm, converting sensations into thoughts, which can then be talked about. The homework, used thoughtfully and appropriately, is a powerful extra string to the therapist's bow.

Through sensate focus, clients have the potential to reconnect with their earliest, somatised memories. This claim is validated by the notion of embodied memory traces. In the preverbal phase, before a child has acquired the capacity to symbolise, experience is organised on a somatosensory level and affects equate to *bodily sensations*. With sensitive mothering, the baby's cognitive capacities develop alongside his increasing command of language, and he begins to express his bodily experience in words (Stolorow & Atwood, 1991). With neglectful or insensitive caregiving and consequent impairment to his development, the infant's affects may fail to progress from bodily states to feelings, and continue to be experienced mostly as bodily states because they have never been able to be symbolised and therefore never articulated. In this scenario, the boundary established between mind and body is such that the experiential domain held in the body remains comparatively large (Krystal, 1988, cited in Stolorow & Atwood, 1991). These theories are similar to Bollas' (1987, p. xv) concept of the "unthought known", in which unsymbolised infantile experiences, that is, "early memories of being and relating", may remain in the unconscious as powerful drivers of emotional-relational responses and behaviour in adult life. These theories also resonate with neuroscientific perspectives that address the part of the unconscious that is not the result of repressing anxiety-laden material (Siegel, 1999). If Winnicott's experiential conglomerate refers to all memories, repressed and non-repressed, pleasurable, painful, or otherwise, then all these embodied memories are potentially recalled by couples in sensate focus.

Using touch to conceptualise unconscious embodied memories

Through the mutual touching carried out at home, couples access many different states simultaneously, and conceptualise their unarticulated, embodied experience. As one psychotherapist said:

> The therapist is going to pick up all sorts of stuff that wouldn't have come out if you'd just been talking.

In all talking therapies, early affective experience needs to be symbolised and put into language, so that it can be discussed and worked through. Whereas in a traditional therapy session a couple can articulate only one thought at a time, the tactile exercises by contrast afford a multitude of affective experiences to be symbolised at once. An important additional point is that in psychoanalysis the preverbal phase of life is regarded as formative in psychosexual development, although the latter may also be impaired by trauma in other phases of life, such as late childhood and adolescence. This point substantiates the proposal that the body holds a number of different non-repressed and repressed states concurrently. For example, one psychotherapist conveyed her understanding of a client's presenting symptom, loss of sexual desire for her husband, when the client reported a repressed memory of her parents' painful separation, which had surfaced in the course of the couple caressing. This therapist stated:

Her father had left her mother . . . and it was her earliest memory,

indicating her interpretation that during the exercises the woman had experienced a powerful paternal transference and overwhelming separation anxiety, which, once made conscious, could be worked through and resolved.

Working with the body through partners' skin-to-skin contact helps practitioners think in new ways about the psychic reality of couples. Is this partly because so much couple interaction is based on procedural knowledge, which is automatic and out of awareness? Procedural knowledge, which is unconscious and hard to access, dictates how human beings relate and defines their expectations of others in relationships. This "implicit relational knowledge", which is essentially psychobiological, mind *and* body, derives from the infant's experience of his environment, mainly his mother's caregiving (Schore, 2012, p. 124):

relational information is transmitted in psychobiological exchanges embedded in the co-created attachment bond. During spontaneous right-brain-to-right-brain visual-facial, auditory-prosodic, and tactile-proprioceptive emotionally charged attachment communications, the sensitive, psychobiologically attuned caregiver regulates, at an implicit level, the infant's states of arousal.

(Schore, 2012, p. 124)

This early interaction forms his world of object relations, encoded gradually in his developing procedural memory system. These internalised sensorimotor models of self-and-other-in-relationship, which unconsciously organise interpersonal behaviour in dysfunctional ways, referred to by Bowlby (1988) as *internal working models*, are the target of change in psychotherapy. It is claimed that change achieved at the level of procedural memory, which is the aim of psychoanalytic psychotherapy, is long-lasting (Fosshage, 2005).

Clients' representations, based on procedural knowledge, are potentially continuously restructured and transformed through adult interaction (Beebe et al., 1997;

Beebe & Lachmann, 2014), which by definition must include psychotherapy. The primary means of accessing unconscious relational models in psychoanalysis is through transference and interpretation. However, some psychoanalysts and psychosexual therapists believe that insight and interpretation as the sole media of change do not necessarily lead to a better or richer sex life for couples. Moreover, it is held among some eminent theorists, for example, by Lyons-Ruth et al. (1998), Wallin (2007) and Schore (2011), that the unsymbolised, implicit (procedural) world is a neglected aspect of psychoanalytic discourse. Other theorists suggest that parent-child interactions encoded in procedural memory are imagistic and not easily translated into symbolic language for linguistic retrieval in adulthood (van der Kolk and van der Hart, 1991; Stern, 1998). Psychotherapists, however, propose that the introduction of sensate focus might make that 'translation' more possible. One experienced couple therapist suggested that:

> you can affect things going on unconsciously by intervening on a behavioural level.

Another senior therapist posited:

> In using the exercises I want to go back to the preverbal senses.

It might be argued therefore that shared touching prescribed by therapists has the potential to bolster access to transferential phenomena.

Exploring the neurobiology of touching and human attachments

Affectionate touch, which is central to the concept of sensate focus, is crucial for the optimal health and well-being of all human beings (Debrot et al., 2021). Loving touch stimulates the release of oxytocin, a peptide hormone and nonapeptide produced in the hypothalamus and released by the posterior pituitary. This hormone is known to play a positive role in effecting relaxation, fearlessness, bonding and contentment in intimate relationships (Brizendine, 2006). It buffers stress, and promotes well-being, social interaction, growth and healing (Uvnäs-Moberg et al., 2022). Originally identified as a female hormone, it is also in males and influences maternal and paternal behaviour in both genetic and non-genetic parents (Carter, 2022). Oxytocin affects reproduction and sexuality, relationships and love, and also helps protect human beings, giving us resilience and the capacity to survive in the world. It is the neuroendocrine foundation of Winnicott's (1968) major concept, primary maternal preoccupation.

Long associated with stimulating labour and milk ejection, oxytocin is released during the continuous psychophysiological interaction between mother and baby in daily life and shapes the infant brain from birth onwards (Gerhardt, 2015). Experiences with caregivers have impact on the neural pathways and create a template for emotional, relational and sexual behaviour in adolescence and adulthood (Hiller, 2022). Daily affectionate skin-to-skin contact is the greatest spur to a baby's development, even more so than breastfeeding, though the two activities are often simultaneous. Generally children who have enjoyed good parenting and physical affection cope well with stress and have a more robust immune system. Loving touch builds the immune system by releasing oxytocin in the lymph system, which protects against inflammation, whereas enduring stress leads to excess cortisol, which affects the lymphocytes in the immune system, making them less responsive. Tender physical affection and warmth induce the reduction of fear and stress-related effects, lowering blood pressure and cortisol levels. Oxytocin is able to reduce the activity of the amygdala, the major fear centre in the brain, and the stress system (Uvnäs-Moberg et al., 2020).

In the frequent and warm skin-to-skin contact experienced between loving mother and baby, positive effects of their shared physical affection are induced in both parent and neonate by an enduring shift in the balance between the oxytocinergic system (the calm and connection system) and the stress system (fight-or-flight response) in favour of the former (Uvnäs-Moberg et al., 2020). In this way positive or negative early experiences contribute to the immune system's strength or fragility, respectively, in later life. Adults who as babies were touched and held often have an abundance of cortisol receptors in the hippocampus, whereas those who were stressed babies, exposed to too much cortisol, have reduced numbers of hippocampal cortisol receptors (Gerhardt, 2015). In such cases, when cortisol levels rise during stressful events and periods in life, and there are fewer receptors to receive it, the cortisol can flood the hippocampus, affecting its growth. In adulthood, a damaged hippocampus is less able to stop the release of further cortisol, which sustains a stressed state of mind. By contrast repeated exposure to oxytocin provides long-lasting benefits to health and well-being (Uvnäs-Moberg et al., 2020).

Whereas infantile experiences that trigger the release of oxytocin are by nature somatosensory, in adulthood the *mental* stimuli of day-to-day social interaction and a creative environment continue to activate the oxytocinergic system with positive benefits, for example, in psychotherapy. Synchronisation, defined as a complex interaction similar to that of psychotherapist and client, whereby the former provides psychological warmth and holding to the latter, promotes oxytocin release and engenders trust and a sense of safety. In therapy, there is an analyst-client affiliative bond, in which behavioural synchrony, autonomic intimacy, oxytocin synchrony and brain-to-brain synchrony are evident (Carter, 2022). These findings underpin Winnicott's seminal concept of the holding environment in clinical work.

Synchrony is in all human relationships where we feel love, safety and intimacy. We need oxytocin to synchronise with others, to relax and restore. The evolution of sociality and love involve a dynamic dance between safety and fear, between oxytocin and its sibling, vasopressin, between approach and avoidance, and between love and fear. Oxytocin supports closeness, whereas vasopressin is more effective in active defence and mobilisation (Carter, 2022).

Aware of the physiological roles that oxytocin and cortisol can play in quality of life, Naruse and Moss (2019, p. 342) suggest that in "healthy but stressed" adult couples, touching (using the authors' "real world" mutual massage programme) provides psychological benefit to partners in the form of reduced feelings of stress and improved coping; a greater sense of well-being, and a strengthening of bonds that consequently enhance affect and mood and improve the overall quality of the relationship. The authors suggest that partners' pleasurable mutual touching is crucial to emotion coregulation, the main focus of their study, and to stress reduction. Even in cases where spouses prefer relational distance, for example, in avoidantly attached couples, touching, even if infrequent, may contribute to a better quality of life and health (Debrot et al., 2021). Interestingly in terms of coping with daily life stress, Brizendine (2006) proposes a significant difference between male and female responses: when women feel stressed, they rebuff affectionate and sexual approaches, whereas for men the opposite may be true. The author asks if this, for women, is because cortisol overrides oxytocin's action in their brain, whereas for men, stress may increase erotic desire and sexual urge. Be that as it may, clinical evidence is that insensitive, anxiety-led, unwanted or painful physical contact kills off desire for intimacy.

In the chapters that follow, psychotherapists' stories of using sensate focus in couple work, their perceived outcomes for those clients, and their thinking behind their decisions not to use it, are supported by neuroendocrine facts outlined in this chapter. When the tactile intervention is introduced into couple psychotherapy and partners are able, with the therapist's support, to enjoy skin-to-skin caressing, they have the potential to discover or rediscover their senses, their sensuality and their pleasure in their bodies. During the tactile exercises the four other senses – sight, sound, smell and taste – play key roles in a couple's experience, just as they contribute to the baby's experience of his mother's care, incorporating in both their shared gaze, affect and co-vocalisation. If regular and tender touch is integrated into partners' lives, it becomes an enduring, replenishing experience enhancing their sense of connection. Sensuous and sensual interaction also has the potential to develop into sexual coupling, if and when partners desire it, or it may simply be enjoyed for its own sake as an investment in the relationship.

Appendix 1

Preface

The focus of this book is the role that sensate focus may play in treating sexual disorders *of all kinds*.

The psychotherapist works to understand the *unique* needs, anxieties and defences of each couple and the emotional-relational forces that drive their sensual-sexual interaction. It is through this understanding, alongside her highly developed self-awareness, that the psychotherapist works appropriately and effectively with sensate focus.

Assessment and understanding of each couple's unique sexual needs and wishes when presenting for therapy are paramount owing to the extensive range of sexual identities as well as non-binary views on gender, which are presented in clinical practice. Today there is no 'normal', only a vast variety in sexual behaviours and goals. Clients' life experience is wide-ranging in terms of ethnicity, cross-cultural partnerships, economic circumstances, education, working environments, expectations of relationships, sexual preferences and orientations, sexual knowledge (some clients lack information about sexual anatomy, for example) and history, gender identities, age, sociocultural forces, life events such as conception, pregnancy and the transition to parenthood, religion, mental health or illness, and physical health and disabilities. The permutations are infinite. This is a far cry from Masters and Johnson's original design of the tactile programme, which targeted white, educated, middle class, married heterosexual couples and concluded with penile-vaginal sexual intercourse. If acceptable in the 1970s, today their design is considered heteronormative.

Having learned the details of the sensate focus programme described subsequently, a reflective psychotherapist modifies each step skilfully, creatively and carefully with the identities and the relationship of the presenting couple at the forefront of her mind. For example, naming the task as 'homework' may evoke powerful transference responses and lead couples to rebel. In these cases, it may be helpful to invite clients to find their own word(s) to describe the exercise task. For couples who cannot immediately broach the first phase, the first task can be made very small, although the concept of "very small" varies widely from couple to couple. Consider inviting partners to start by doing a 'rehearsal', simply preparing a room, nothing more.

Finally, psychotherapists do not generally give written copies of these guidelines to clients. In 30 years' clinical experience, I have only been asked twice for a written copy of the programme. In neither case did the couple read it. This fact speaks volumes.

Couple caressing exercises (sensate focus) – ground rules and guidelines for psychotherapists

The psychotherapist invites clients to do the following:

Agree with their partner not to have sexual intercourse or genital touching, or orgasm for this early phase of sensate focus.

Set up appointments with each other, to help them make a time commitment for the exercises and protect their couple space. In this way, partners have equal responsibility and neither partner has to take the initiative.

Try not to 'squeeze' the appointments in between other planned events; leave plenty of free time before and after the exercises.

To feel fresh and relaxed, they may wish to have a bath or shower beforehand, but that is not essential.

Avoid talking during the exercise, so that they focus on their sense of touch.

Preferably avoid music and candles.

Choose a room for the exercise, which may or may not be their bedroom.

Create a very warm room, especially if they have agreed to be fully naked together without bedcoverings. Extra heating is needed, because the body temperature tends to drop as they relax. If they feel more comfortable wearing some item of clothing, that is fine.

Choose a room in which they feel safe.

Ensure privacy, which is essential if they are to focus on each other and not be distracted by family, pets or phones.

Remember that the goal of these exercises is to learn how to be present in the moment, how to be inside their own bodies.

Notice what they are thinking, feeling and sensing each time they do this exercise, so that the three of you may discuss their responses in the next therapy session.

Phase 1

Taking plenty of time, each person explores the other's naked body (if being naked is comfortable for both partners) by stroking and caressing, avoiding breasts, buttocks and genitals, and avoiding trying to make the other feel a certain way. Focus on their sense of touch and on their own experience (whether giving or receiving) during the first phase.

Start with a maximum of 5 minutes per side per person (it may be less), increasing from a total of 20 minutes to 40 minutes (10 minutes per side), then to 60 minutes (15 minutes per side) over several weeks during the first phase.

Avoid talking during the exercise, except to tell their partner when or if a particular touch is painful or unacceptable; at such points, if there are any, the person doing the caressing stops and moves on to a different area of the body or begins to touch the other in a different, acceptable way. Reports of tickling and massaging suggest that partners' touch is too light and too deep, respectively, and are to be avoided.

Remember that each person is responsible for his or her own feelings, whatever they are.

Also note that this touching is not intended to be erotic.

Take it in turns to give first, because the experiences of giving first and giving second are different.

Make sure they find a comfortable position for doing the touching. If possible, try not to 'break' the hand-to-body contact too often.

After a few weeks of phase 1, some familiarity with the exercise and trust might allow them to include the breasts and nipples of both partners, without attempting to stimulate their partner, and to begin to experiment with a variety of touches, sensations and experiences, such as talcum powder, body oils, feathers, silks or other fabrics.

Continue as above, and start requesting the types of touch they prefer.

Now both partners are lying on their side, so that the person being touched can easily guide the hand of the person touching. (In this position one person faces the back of the head of the other.)

Phase 2

Maintain their agreement not to have sexual intercourse.

Start to include genital touching as part of the exercise already established, so there are now no 'no go' areas of their bodies.

Be creative in their caressing, in pace and pattern.

Continuing all the above, concentrate more on the genitals to discover the sensations resulting from different but gentle pressures in different areas.

There is an optional further stage of mutual masturbation to orgasm, either stimulating themselves or being stimulated by their partner. Do the caressing first and then the genital stimulation at the end. Take turns, so that each partner can focus on their sensations; avoid trying for simultaneous orgasm.

Maintaining the exclusion of sexual intercourse, continue as before, working at an appropriate pace as agreed with the therapist.

Options for heterosexual couples:

The man starts to rub his erect penis along his partner's genitals, without vaginal entry.

The next step is containment without movement, allowing the penis, centimetre by centimetre, to be contained by the vagina. (Use lubricant if it enhances the experience.) This stage is known as 'quiet vagina', or vaginal containment.
Continue the containment and start to add gentle thrusting and rotating movements.

Options for same-sex couples:

Do the caressing as in previous stages. Include the contact and activity that they have found to be the most pleasurable.

If desired, they discuss and agree their preferred ways of erotic stimulation and continue to orgasm if that is their goal.

References

Bancroft, J. (2008) *Human sexuality and its problems*. 3rd edn. Edinburgh: Churchill Livingstone.

Beebe, B. and Lachmann, F.M. (2014) *The origins of attachment. Infant research and adult treatment*. Hove: Routledge.

Beebe, B., Lachmann, F.M. and Jaffe, J. (1997) 'A transformational model of presymbolic representations: Reply to commentaries', *Psychoanalytic Dialogues*, 7(2), pp. 215–224. https://doi.org/10.1080/10481889709539177

Belliveau, F. and Richter, L. (1970) *Understanding "Human sexual inadequacy"*. Boston: Little, Brown and Company.

Berry, M.D. (2013) 'The history and evolution of sex therapy and its relationship to psychoanalysis', *International Journal of Applied Psychoanalytic Studies*, 10(1), pp. 53–74. https://doi.org/10.1002/aps.1315

Berry, M.D. (2014) *Towards a psychodynamically-informed model for the integrative psychotherapeutic treatment of male sexual dysfunction*. PhD thesis, University College London [Online]. http://ethos.bl.uk (Accessed: 3 February 2016).

Bollas, C. (1987) *The shadow of the object. Psychoanalysis of the unthought known*. London: Free Association Books.

Bowlby, J. (1988) *A secure base. Clinical applications of attachment theory*. London: Routledge.

Brizendine, L. (2006) *The female brain*. New York: Morgan Road Books.

Brooks, S. (1994) 'Treating inhibited sexual desire: the intersystem model', in Weeks, G.R. and Hof, L. (eds.) *The marital-relationship therapy casebook*. New York: Brunner Mazel, pp. 149–168.

Carter, S. (2022) 'Oxytocin and love: myths and mysteries', in *Oxytocin: The neurobiological mystery of love and attachment*. London: Confer.

Debrot, A., Stellar, J.E., MacDonald, G., Keltner, D. and Impett, E.A. (2021) 'Is touch in romantic relationships universally beneficial for psychological well-being? The role of attachment avoidance', *Personality and Social Psychology Bulletin*, 47(10), pp. 1495–1509. https://doi.org/10.1177/0146167220977709

Fosshage, J.L. (2005) 'The explicit and implicit domains in psychoanalytic change', *Psychoanalytic Inquiry*, 25(4), pp. 516–539. https://doi.org/10.2513/s07351690pi2504_7

Freud, S. (1900–1901) 'The interpretation of dreams (second part)', in *Standard edition 5*. London: The Hogarth Press and the Institute of Psychoanalysis, pp. 339–626.

Gerhardt, S. (2015) *Why love matters*. 2nd edn. London: Routledge.

Hawton, K. (1993) *Sex therapy. A practical guide*. Oxford: Oxford University Press.

Hiller, J. (2022) 'Developmental deprivation, oxytocin and the couple relationship', in *Oxytocin: the neurobiological mystery of love and attachment*. London: Confer.

Hunter, J. (1786) *A treatise on venereal disease*. London: St George's Hospital Medical School.

Iasenza, S. (2001) 'Sex therapy with "A new view"', in Kaschak, E. and Tiefer, L. (eds.) *A new view of women's sexual problems*. New York: Haworth Press, pp. 43–46.

Kaplan, H.S. (1987) *The illustrated manual of sex therapy*. 2nd edn. New York: Brunner Mazel.

Kolodny, R.C. (1981) 'Evaluating sex therapy: Process and outcome at the Masters & Johnson Institute', *The Journal of Sex Research*, 17(4), pp. 301–318. https://doi.org/10.1080/00224498109551123

Krystal, H. (1988) *Integration and self-healing: Affect, trauma, alexithymia*. London: Routledge.

Lazarus, A.A. (1965) 'The treatment of a sexually inadequate man', in Ullmann, L.P. and Krasner, L. (eds.) *Case studies in behavior modification*. New York: Holt, Rinehart and Winston, pp. 243–260.

Levine, S.B. (2009) 'I am not a sex therapist!', *Archives of Sexual Behavior*, 38(6), pp. 1033–1034. https://doi.org/10.1007/s10508-009-9474-x

Linschoten, M., Weiner, L. and Avery-Clark, C. (2016) 'Sensate focus: A critical literature review', *Sexual and Relationship Therapy*, 31(2), pp. 230–246. https://doi.org/10.1080/14681994.2015.1127909

LoPiccolo, J. (1994) 'The evolution of sex therapy', *Sexual and Marital Therapy*, 9(1), pp. 5–7. https://doi.org/10.1080/02674659408409562

Lyons-Ruth, K., Bruschweiler-Stern, N., Harrison, A.M., Morgan, A.C., Nahum, J.P., Sander, L., Stern, D.N. and Tronick, E.Z. (1998) 'Implicit relational knowing: Its role in development and psychoanalytic treatment', *Infant Mental Health Journal*, 19(3), pp. 282–289. https://doi.org/10.1002/(SICI)1097-0355(199823)19:3<282::AID-IMHJ3>3.0.CO;2-O

Masters, W.H. and Johnson, V.E. (1970) *Human sexual inadequacy*. Boston: Little, Brown & Co.

Morgan, M. (2019) *A couple state of mind. Psychoanalysis of couples and the Tavistock Relationships model*. Abingdon: Routledge.

Naruse, S.M. and Moss, M. (2019) 'Effects of couples positive massage programme on well-being, perceived stress and coping, and relation satisfaction', *Health Psychology and Behavioral Medicine*, 7(1), pp. 328–347. https://doi.org/10.1080/21642850.2019.1682586.

Ogden, T.H. (1994) 'The concept of interpretive action', *Psychoanalytic Quarterly*, 63(2), pp. 219–245. https://doi.org/10.1080/21674086.1994.11927413

Scharff, D.E. and Savege Scharff, J. (1991) *Object relations couple therapy*. London: Jason Aronson.

Schnarch, D. (1997) *Passionate marriage: keeping love and intimacy alive in committed relationships*. London: W W Norton.

Schore, A.N. (2011) 'The right brain implicit self lies at the core of psychoanalysis', *Psychoanalytic Dialogues*, 21(1), pp. 75–100. https://doi.org/10.1080/10481885.2011.545329

Schore, A.N. (2012) *The science of the art of psychotherapy*. London: W.W. Norton.

Siegel, D.J. (1999) *The developing mind*. New York: The Guilford Press.

Stern, D.N. (1998) *The interpersonal world of the infant*. 2nd edn. London: Karnac.

Stolorow, R.D. and Atwood, G.E. (1991) 'The mind and the body', *Psychoanalytic Dialogues*, 1(2), pp. 181–195. https://doi.org/10.1080/10481889109538892

The Daily Telegraph (2013) Obituaries. *Virginia Johnson*, 27 July, p. 27.

Tiefer, L. (1995) *Sex is not a natural act*. Boulder: Westview Press.

Uvnäs-Moberg, K., Handlin, L. and Petersson, M. (2020) 'Neuroendocrine mechanisms involved in the physiological effects caused by skin-to-skin contact – With a particular focus on the oxytocinergic system', *Infant Behavior and Development*, 61. https://doi.org/10.1016/j.infbeh.2020.101482

Uvnäs-Moberg, K., Julius, H., Handlin, L. and Petersson, M. (2022) 'Editorial: Sensory stimulation and oxytocin: Their roles in social interaction and health promotion', *Front Psychology*, 13. https://doi.org/10.3389/fpsyg.2022.929741

van der Kolk, B.A. and van der Hart, O. (1991) 'The intrusive past: the flexibility of memory and the engraving of trauma', *American Imago*, 48(4), pp. 425–454.

Wallin, D.J. (2007) *Attachment in psychotherapy*. New York: Guilford Press.

Weeks, G.R., Gambescia, N. and Hertlein, K.M. (2016) *A clinician's guide to systemic sex therapy*. 2nd edn. New York: Routledge.

Weiner, L. and Avery-Clark, C. (2014) 'Sensate focus: Clarifying the Masters and Johnson's model', *Sexual and Relationship Therapy*, 29(3), pp. 307–319. https://doi.org/10.1080/14681994.2014.892920

Weiner, L. and Avery-Clark, C. (2017) *Sensate focus in sex therapy. The illustrated manual*. Abingdon: Routledge.

Winnicott, D.W. (1964) 'The child and sex', *The child, the family, and the outside world*. London: Penguin Books, pp. 147–160.

Winnicott, D.W. (1968) 'Communication between infant and mother, and mother and infant, compared and contrasted', in Joffe, W.G. (ed.) *What is psychoanalysis?* London: Institute of Psychoanalysis, pp. 15–25.

Wolpe, J. (1958) *Psychotherapy by reciprocal inhibition*. Stanford, CA: Stanford University Press.

Zeitner, R. (2013) *Email to Susan Pacey*, 3 June.

Chapter 4

Embodying

Reflecting on the emotional impact of sensate focus

At first glance the steps and phases of the sensate focus programme may look simple to anyone, therapist or client, new to the process. The reality is that each task has the potential to evoke both loving and traumatic experiences from very early life and to have significant effects. For this reason, experienced psychotherapists tread carefully before introducing the concept into clinical work, reflecting extensively on their reasons and motivation for using this particular intervention and on the couple's dynamics and stage of development.

In this regard, an early, memorable lesson for me came from my training course in psychosexual therapy. As trainees we were supervised in small groups of four co-therapists. On one occasion our group supervisor asked us all to do sensate focus, phase 1, step 1, with our partners at home and report on our experience in the next session. Peals of laughter rang out, perhaps voicing both excitement and anxiety, and one supervisee insisted that the supervisor do the exercise, too. Was this a precursor of the power dynamics mobilised in the therapy? We all agreed and gave our reports in the following session. It would be inappropriate to disclose all our reactions before, during and after doing the homework; suffice it to say that our errors of omission in critical guidelines and misunderstandings with our partners led to wide-ranging outcomes from anger, conflict, feelings of disappointment, through to surprise, warmth and pleasure.

At this early point in my career as a psychotherapist the crucial learning was the extraordinary range of sensations and emotions the task evoked in group members and their spouses, experiences that would later be reported by my clients in similar and new ways. It was also invaluable to gain a sense of and respect for the significant professional responsibility involved in inviting couples to share affective and sensual interaction as part of the treatment. A golden rule now for me is not to underestimate the power of sensate focus and to consider carefully and over time its potential impact on the couple before introducing even the very idea of it into the therapy.

DOI: 10.4324/9781003328292-4

Creating a place of safety: the holding environment

In Chapter 1, I stated that this book is intended to help practitioners think about the clinical ramifications of introducing sensate focus, the 'if and when' of this intervention being a judgement call for every clinician. Long before the tactile programme emerges in the therapist's mind as a possibly helpful intervention in couple work, a good working alliance between therapist and client needs to be in place. The processes of building a relationship of trust, protection and reliability with both partners, and over time helping them to learn to trust each other, are crucial. Without trust the therapeutic endeavour is fruitless. The analyst-couple relationship is the key instrument of positive emotional-relational change in clients, and that holds true with or without sensate focus. The therapeutic alliance is universally acknowledged as the first clinical task in all schools of psychotherapy. It was Donald Winnicott (1955a) who first proposed that the professional relationship *is* the therapy. His concept became, and is still, accepted wisdom in our field (Fonagy, 1999). Winnicott explains how in certain ways the task of the therapist is similar to that of parents. As he (Winnicott, 1963a, p. 340) suggests, "Psychoanalysis . . . is not at all like child care . . . But . . . there is nothing we [analysts] do that is unrelated to child care and infant-care". For Winnicott (1955b), the analyst provides a holding environment to her client, as do ordinary parents to their infants. A baby's development is heavily reliant on the quality of his *environmental provision*, his mother's love and caregiving (this is a given for most infants), thanks to his good enough mother and her daily, moment-by-moment adaptation to her infant's needs (Winnicott, 1960). In both parenting and therapy, when attunement is imperfect, as inevitably it is on occasions, some positive development can take place. In this way imperfections in care, if well managed, can be turned into growth points for infants and adult clients alike.

In the context of this book, the multidimensional concept of holding (Winnicott, 1955b) is particularly apt. In psychotherapy the psychological aspects of holding involve certain personal qualities in the therapist, who is more reliable than other people, who focusses on her client's needs, who communicates an understanding of her client's narrative and who conveys genuine caring. These qualities are expressed through a positive, authentic interest in the client as well as by maintaining strict start and finish times of sessions. All these aspects of a holding environment create a highly specialised professional setting, in which couples may feel safe enough to talk about their relationships and disclose their anxieties. Inevitably the therapist observes transference and countertransference phenomena emerging in the sessions; these help her identify the couple's unmet needs from early life. If introduced into the clinical work, sensate focus brings the other side of holding into the therapy, that is the physical. Touching is two-way; a person cannot touch another without also being touched. Such contact between partners is likely to evoke infantile, tactile experience of being handled and held by caregivers.

A key message of this book is this: before introducing sensate focus into the clinical work, the therapist needs to assess carefully whether a couple have achieved enough emotional growth *either* to undertake the first task, *or* to be able to think about the experience of *not* doing it, if the partners agreed to do it in the previous session.

The first question for the analyst therefore is whether the couple, although vulnerable, have begun to build up a shared belief in a protective, benign and safe environment. According to Winnicott (1958), clients' development of a sense of safety equates to Melanie Klein's concept of introjecting a good object. At this stage, the therapist considers whether a couple have enough confidence and trust to engage in the homework in a bounded way, particularly as the therapist (the mother) is going to be physically absent. If the therapist (mother) has been internalised as a good object by the partners, she can still be "felt" even when she cannot be seen (Wright, 1991, p. 76). In this way holding and feeling held extend to the couple's home. Another theoretical perspective, that of Morgan's (2019, p. xxii) "couple state of mind", is valuable in this context. The therapist's capacity to hold a couple state of mind is important and containing for clients, because the therapist's focus is the relationship that the partners create together, as well as each partner's own intrapsychic and interpersonal world. According to Morgan, adopting a couple state of mind means being able to think about the couple dynamics from a metaposition, a 'third area'. In her view, couples present for therapy unable to think about each person's subjectivity and how they both have a part in the relationship they have created. If one partner of a couple in treatment is regarded as at fault and to blame for the other's unhappiness, the other partner may expect the therapist to help change the errant spouse's behaviour. In these cases, a couple state of mind is missing: the spouses cannot observe and think about their relationship as a joint endeavour, either positively or negatively. An important goal of couple psychotherapy is that partners internalise the therapist's model of the capacity to observe themselves and each other interacting, that is in relationship.

Ideally before embarking on sensate focus all these considerations would be in the practitioner's mind, but not necessarily achieved. However, when this type of assessment is challenging and substantial doubts about using the tactile intervention prevail, a secure practitioner is cautious, waits a while, mulls it over and maybe discusses the pros and cons in supervision, putting the caressing programme on hold for review later in the therapy.

Accessing anxieties about sexuality

The first tactile exercises may act as a diagnostic tool for couple psychotherapists whose goal is to access clients' unconscious emotions and patterns of attachment arising from early relationships with parents or caregivers. When observing in the session how their clients report their experience of doing the homework, for example, by noting their body language, tone of voice and choice of words, therapists can help partners explore connections between their experience of touching as adults and their hitherto unconscious experiences of being handled and held in their mother's arms during infancy. The value of clients' first reports was conveyed strongly in my doctoral study: therapists seemed to be much less concerned with adhering to or working through the traditional step-by-step programme as such; rather they used the early basic exercises to start to build an in-depth understanding of individuals' preverbal, embodied experiences. As one therapist said:

> I'm not going to ask how many times did you do the homework, how many minutes was it and how did you feel when he touched you? You know, it's more like, "So, what's happening in this process for you guys?" So when I do use it, I think ... well, I think the body gets missed sometimes in therapy, the kind of bodily skin-on-skin stuff and how we understand what's happened to people at a skin level, infantile stuff. And I think sometimes if you can use aspects of sensate focus it can help people get back in touch, or get in touch with something of that.

The significance of the homework appeared to be in bringing to the surface how touching and nakedness, essential elements of the exercises, enable partners to know about their own primitive fears of tactile intimacy and learn to bear their fears. Clients may then begin to understand their acute sense of vulnerability when seen and caressed by another person. Whatever the responses of the couple, each partner's feelings can then be acknowledged verbally by the therapist and as a result both spouses may develop a greater awareness and understanding of their unconscious anxieties held until then in their implicit memory:

> It's about learning what your responses are and understanding yourself in the presence of another. And so it's ... it's really about that, and it's not about technique or anything else. It is about lowering anxiety; it is about learning how to be vulnerable. And ... one of the valuable things I still think about sensate focus is that it allows people to understand how scared they are of their vulnerability in the face of their bareness, one with the other, their nakedness. Yeah, that's kind of why I find it useful. I think it's always very interesting when couples start it and they come up against how scared they get in the therapy and in their homework.

Sometimes introducing the programme as an idea rather than a task shifts the couple dynamics and opens new avenues for exploration. The mere act of speaking about sensate focus might have different, helpful effects on couples. For example, in the case vignette below, it seems that introducing the touching exercises mobilised anxieties and defences in both partners, which the therapist could then address. An important second consideration is this: the act of describing the tool was 'permission-giving' to the couple, whose thoughts about the homework had mobilised their shame ("You want us to do *what*?"). The therapist's thinking and talking about the partners' mutual caressing helped detoxify their overwhelming shame and encouraged them to start speaking about sex, which even in today's sexualised society remains taboo for some people:

> Sensate focus feels like an aspect of therapy that gets integrated when it makes sense. A lot of times I'm doing it without the behavioural piece, just using,

planting the idea of it, the thinking about it, "If you were to do this, what would happen?" And . . . em . . . well, you don't really have to do sensate focus, because it's the *idea* of doing it that gets the dynamics going with the couple and you end up working with their resistance, but then some people are very modest and have so much shame: "You want us to do *what*?" So maybe they do a little bit of it, or . . . have a try, or they get a taste . . . in their minds at least, anyway.

In summary, introducing the tactile intervention may help clients think about and discuss their difficult responses in sensual, intimate environments, especially those individuals who find it hard to articulate their feelings, and provide an alternative channel of emotional-relational communication. That said, the therapist needs to distinguish between clients who cannot express their emotions and might be helped by this approach, and those who can talk about their feelings but refuse to disclose them in the session. The refusal to be open may be a symptom of hostility in the couple and contraindicate sensate focus. This scenario is discussed in Chapter 5.

As couples engage in the homework, they may recall distressing events from the past, which may then be linked to their current sexual problems. These are very powerful, cathartic moments in therapy. Sometimes the exercises may be stopped at these points to allow clients to recall the details of and work through the trauma. Below is an example of a couple presenting with loss of desire. The therapist describes how the touching exercises brought a traumatic memory sharply back into the woman's awareness:

> She was very concerned that she'd gone off him, very distressed and slightly panicked by her loss of desire for him. And the level of her distress was hard to understand and only became clear after I set them sensate focus. And the first time they did it, it was fine. And the following week it was okay, but there was a real reticence on her part. And then it emerged that her father had left her mother when she was two and a half, and it was her earliest memory. She remembers the whole thing of the father with the suitcase, the mother holding onto his leg and just standing there, crying and crying, and then the mother crying and crying and crying. So what happens if you're not sexual enough? Does the man leave? What happens if you don't fancy your partner? Do you leave? In other words, her loss of desire was somehow catastrophic. And so I stopped the exercises because it had brought up something that was much more important to think about.

From the therapist's perspective, sensate focus helped bring repressed trauma into the client's consciousness, so that it could be talked about, understood and resolved.

Occasionally a therapist may even use the homework in the expectation that the couple will *not* do it, but come to the next session more open about themselves and more willing to discuss their predicament:

> The couple might be saying, "If only we had sex, it would be fine". If then they try to do the first sensate focus exercises, the chances are they will come back

not able to engage with that and more open to thinking about what might be going on.

A common thread running through practitioners' stories of sensate focus was its usefulness in cases where partners said that the quality of their emotional relationship had improved significantly but they still could not have sex. This phenomenon may arise when the couple have not had sex for a long time, maybe several years. That said, not all spouses who have a good enough companionate relationship want to resume sex. They might, or they might not. In cases where verbal therapy alone has not translated into sexual change in the couple and where the partners, having a shared desire to resume sex, express disappointment, the touching exercises may help them surmount their defences:

> Because sexual behaviour is physical, clients get completely frozen, so they might be able to understand where it's coming from, how it's developed, what the problem is, but it doesn't necessarily help them to change it. And that's where sensate focus can be incredibly useful in giving clients a safe, boundaried way to proceed and engage, sensually as well as sexually.

Although psychotherapy is often called "the talking cure", in some cases too much talking without pause for breath, thought or input from others can serve as an avoidance of contact. The case vignette below is an example of a couple using talk as an impenetrable defence, which the therapist addresses through the touching exercises:

> I think doing it bodily for her has shown her something that talking couldn't; she could talk a blue streak, they talk all the time. They say they communicate, and I'm not sure how much they really do. And I think that's what the space without words is about in sensate focus. They learn, they're learning how to stay in themselves more at a physical, bodily level without the anxiousness of talking and talking and talking and talking.

In this way, the psychotherapist uses the first phase of the programme to illuminate problematic emotional aspects of the couple's relationship through a physical route, and to help partners access their vulnerability. In clinical work couples often present with fantasies of a seamless experience in sex and their discontent at their failure to achieve it. The quotation below describes how owing to the partners' apparent frustration, the therapist had given them "something to do" to address their problem (a scenario discussed further in Chapter 5); they then struggled with and were defeated by an idealised expectation of a flawless sensual experience:

> They haven't been having any sexual contact for quite a while, and she's got tired of initiating. He's quite passive. And a lot of our work has been about that process, her expectations of him, and him hiding, metaphorically or physically,

from her upset. One way or another he's in the doghouse. Then they were very clear about it, they said, "We would like something that we can do, so we feel we're doing something". So we are sitting for the past three months at sensate focus one. Not moving on, because they're finding it very difficult. And so they're learning quite a lot about what it is that they are . . . hiding from through not doing, not setting it up, setting it up but finding it a bit boring . . . quite liking it but her being in tears because she shouldn't have to be doing it this way. And I think that the learning is that she doesn't want to have to negotiate the difference, the space between them at all. And what's interesting about sensate focus is that you can actually get to something like that.

Thinking about sexual anxiety and the capacity to be in the moment

Generally the goal of sensate focus in the early phase is the development of a couple's capacity for intimacy in the form of shared caressing and relaxation when naked and vulnerable in the presence of another person. This relaxed mode seems to be captured exquisitely by Winnicott's (1962) theory of unintegration, which incorporates at once the ability to relax in an unexcited state and a developmental achievement in both infant *and* adult, since it implies an ability to trust and feel at one with the environment. In healthy development, the quiet states of the very young, totally dependent infant involve his ability to rest without feeling a push to integrate. This state is assured by his mother's holding, which supports his immature ego. Unintegration is simply *being*, according to Winnicott (1987, p. 12), who proposes that *being* is the "beginning of everything"; a continuity of going-on-being is needed by the baby in a quantity "enough to establish the self that is eventually a person". Paradoxically the ability to regress to an unintegrated state is a mark of maturity, of successful integration, and of the development of a unit self, in which:

> the skin becomes the boundary between the me and not-me. In other words, the psyche has come to live in the soma and an individual psychosomatic life has been initiated.
>
> (Winnicott, 1962, p. 61)

If, however, the mother's holding is inadequate and the baby suffers gross impingements on his going-on-being, he disintegrates, a reaction which is both frightening *and* a sophisticated defence created by the infant against his fears of annihilation (Winnicott, 1968).

Occasionally therapists observe a degree of disintegration in their clients' responses to sensate focus (implying that partial integration had taken place in the past). They are managing couples' multiple, complex, primitive anxieties simultaneously. Importantly, by introducing the tactile exercises, a therapist is effectively inviting partners to recreate a problematic sexual and emotional-relational experience together at home. In some cases, the absence of sex might have led to a psychological and sexual distancing in the relationship, possibly after years of avoiding physical contact with one another, as discussed earlier. Inevitably therapists expect couples' sexual anxieties to emerge immediately and continue to surface during the process: "it allows people to understand how scared they are of their vulnerability in the face of their bareness . . . one with the other".

Analysts hold in mind the need to balance support and challenge, giving support as a good object against partners' inevitable fears evoked by the exercises. A tolerable level of anxiety might help partners be curious about themselves and build their capacity to reflect on their experience (Clulow, 2017). How might analysts achieve that balance? Respondents in my study distinguished between two scenarios: firstly, a couple losing a previous state of equilibrium and so experiencing anxiety associated with this pressure to change; and secondly, a couple being in a state of uncertainty and open to influence. The following scenario shows this kind of challenge:

> I had one case where the woman was having body memories in the sensate focus exercises and remembering inappropriate touching and really freaked out in the moment and pushed him away. So it was good that they could come in and talk through what had happened, because he felt so traumatised by her trauma. "I didn't hurt her", he said. She had remembered a sort of a coming-from-behind experience, not sexually but a touching by someone behind her, a somatised memory. Back in the therapy room she was able to piece it together. It threw them for a while. But it was healing for him to know that it wasn't about him; that realisation healed his shame about being a bad boy for wanting to touch her. After a while they could discuss how they could make doing sensate focus safe for them both and that discussion led to them being able to do it.

In this case a client's recovery of an intrusive, possibly abusive, somatised memory retraumatised both partners. The therapist conveyed her understanding of their defensive reaction to a powerful impingement on their going-on-being. For the couple, disintegration and chaos ensued ("It threw them for a while"). The therapist explained how her interpretation of the couple's transference to each other enabled the partners' experience to be symbolised and repaired ("he felt a bad boy . . . so it was healing for him to know it wasn't about him"). Importantly, by doing the exercises, the couple connected to their own infantile experience as well as learning about their partner's. It seemed that after the initial disintegration, the therapist's holding enabled her clients to learn to 'parent' themselves and each other. They then became creative together in negotiating their own holding environment. This meant psychologically holding and being held by the other, so that they might feel safe enough to share the tactile exploration ("After a while they could discuss how to make sensate focus safe for them both and that discussion led to them being able to do it"). For Winnicott (1992), play starts as a symbol of the infant's trust in the mother, just as in this case vignette, the therapist believed that sensate focus could be broached when the couple could trust her *and* each other.

These quotations highlight couples' interaction symbolically in terms of their early experience of their mother's handling during breast-feeding and their primary identification with the breast. At this stage the baby and breast are one and the same; that is, the baby feels merged with his mother and the breast is felt by the infant to be under his omnipotent control (Winnicott, 1971a). The couple below illustrate that primitive phase:

> The man liked to cross-dress and it was an important part of arousal for him. Working with how that could be integrated within the sexual relationship in a way that didn't feel too intrusive for *her*, but was sufficiently arousing for *him*, was a very helpful part of the process of sensate focus. There was a disjunction but not a dysfunction, and going through sensate focus enabled them to talk about their feelings about it, both positive and negative.

According to Winnicott (1971a, pp. 81–82), the maternal breast has male and female elements, something that the male partner in the previous illustration may have been struggling to integrate:

> The male element *does* [italics in original], while the female element *is*. . . . Either the mother has a breast that *is*, so that the baby can also *be* when the baby and mother are not yet separated out in the infant's rudimentary mind; or else the mother is incapable of making this contribution, in which case the baby has to develop without the capacity to be, or with a crippled capacity to be. Clinically one deals with a baby who has to make do with an identity with a breast that is active, which is a male element breast, but which is not satisfactory for the initial identity which needs a breast that *is*, not a breast that *does*.

The tactile exercises can facilitate couples' capacity just to *be*, relaxed in each other's presence, together in a state of unintegration without impingements or intrusions on their going-on-being. Hewison (2017) proposes that Winnicott's notion of "first the being, then the doing" can be translated into the "being" of the couple relationship and then the "doing" of the partners within it. A couple's relaxed, non-active state (their being) enables their creativity (their doing) in discussing how to integrate each other's needs into their sexual relationship. Interestingly, Winnicott (1964b, p. 146) links play and the true self with dressing in adulthood:

> Play can be 'a being honest about oneself', just as dressing can be for an adult.

Helping couples develop

Repairing shame

> It's very vulnerable to be lying there with no clothes on and to be touched by your partner and perhaps that can bring up anxieties and whether you can show your partner your vulnerabilities. It's about sharing difficult stuff.

Shame is a universal phenomenon that can have a significant negative impact on clients' sexual relationships. The links between shame, sexuality and sociocultural sexual taboos are well established in the literature (Nathanson, 1987; Mollon, 2005; Lichtenberg, 2008; Clulow, 2009). A degree of shame is necessary for an individual's socialisation and that is healthy. However, unregulated, debilitating shame, sometimes referred to as toxic shame, dampens desire and arousal in couples. Although the act of 'bringing themselves to therapy' may in itself be shaming for clients as soon as they walk into the consulting room, this affect is more likely to emerge and be amplified in the physical intimacy and nakedness of the homework. Against this, the tactile exercises may also metabolise toxic shame, thereby enhancing partners' capacity for shared sensual expression.

The full force of debilitating shame can emerge in the context of partners' anxieties about being naked together. Theorist, psychoanalyst and neuroscientist Allan Schore helps clinicians make sense of the inhibiting impact of this affect. Drawing on Winnicottian concepts, Schore (1998) asserts that phenomenologically clients experience shame as a discontinuity, a disruption to their going-on-being. This claim places the roots of shame at the beginning of life prior to the achievement of a psychosomatic existence, when inadequate maternal care might compromise the infant's attainment of "psychosomatic indwelling" (Winnicott, 1960, p. 589). A failure of indwelling in infancy might be manifested in adult couples as defensiveness against unconscious intolerable conflicts over their needs for tenderness, bodily contact and sexual play within a world experienced as rejecting, an experience repeated in the transference operating between partners (Stolorow & Atwood, 1991). Discontinuity might also lead to a client feeling that his body is flawed, his defective body concretising the rejected, unacceptable self (Stolorow & Atwood, 1991).

Primitive shaming experiences are thought to be compounded by humiliating parental sanctions and prohibitions in the second year of life and beyond, as caregivers attempt to socialise their children (Schore, 1998; Lichtenberg, 2008). Of note, Schore (2012) argues that the affect of shame is central to human development: he claims that shame tolerance, the ability to consciously experience the narcissistic pain of shame, is a healthy prerequisite to establishing a positive self-belief and a valuing of the self. By contrast unregulated or toxic shame is an unconscious, potent shame, which drives the process of repression and inhibits an individual's emotional development by deactivating the innate maturational drive (Schore, 2012). Susceptibility to shame is associated with a history of abuse (Gilbert, 1998), as described in this vignette:

I'm thinking of one client in particular, who didn't feel comfortable with her partner being naked and then we worked out why, making the link to an angry, authoritarian father who shouted at her when as a child she saw him naked. She is now able to cope with her own nakedness and her partner's, but she keeps a shawl close by, which she can throw over herself if she feels a moment's jitter.

So in this case might the practitioner be thinking about the shawl as a defence and protection (possibly symbolically the mother's body) against a frightening *and* shaming paternal object? The woman's automatic defensive act, to cover herself with a shawl when anxious, may have been her protection against shame as much as her fear of her partner when naked (her father in the transference).

Some psychotherapists use sensate focus to detoxify a range of shaming experiences in couples' early lives. The goal is to help couples learn to regulate their unregulated shame and build their capacity for pleasurable sensuality, modifying negative body representations. The theme of discovering the pleasure of sensuality permeates the case vignettes in this book. In this respect, the vignettes reflect Lichtenberg's (2008) proposal, which is that healthy adult sexuality is built on the platform of infantile enjoyment of sensual experiences. This notion recalls Winnicott's (1963b, p. 76) description of the "sensuous co-existence" of mother and baby. For Lichtenberg (2008, p. 19), sexual goals in adults "represent a struggle between body pleasure-seeking arousal and the inhibiting force of shame". If children's expression of sensuous excitement incurs their parents' disapproval (according to parents' own sociocultural attitudes and unconscious procedural memories) *and* is met with parental insensitivity, then pleasurable experience may be converted in the infant's mind as something disgusting and humiliating (Clulow, 2017).

The association of shame with the felt need to disappear, to be invisible, to hide and not be seen is manifest in clinical work. In the context of shame, sensuality and body representation, vision may be as important as touch in the reparative role of sensate focus. This brings to mind Winnicott's (1967, p. 111) seminal concept of the "mirror role" of the mother and the importance of the infant's experience of "being seen" and loved by his caregiver, an intersubjective experience promoting his personality growth and creative capacity. According to Winnicott (1967, p. 113), during the psychophysical maternal holding, the baby "gets back what he is giving, and he sees himself in the mother's face . . . 'en rapport' with her". This is similar to the psychotherapeutic process, when the client sees (and feels) the therapist's understanding and care. Mirroring is a two-way process, in which the infant's personality develops and his world is enriched with meaning; it is an early nonverbal form of symbolisation. For Wright (2009, p. 143, italics in original) these pre-symbolic, nonverbal exchanges form the essential building blocks of psychic structure:

> Each discrete expression resonates with a discrete infant state and provides an image of it. In this sense, the infant *discovers himself* in the mother's response, and . . . finds in the medium of her face an external form for his own feeling.

If mother and baby are not 'en rapport', that is, with little mutuality, the baby only sees the mother's face as an uninvolved object that may be looked at, but is not engaged with his experience. In this case, if the mother is narcissistically preoccupied, she may not be available to mirror her infant's experience, conveying only her mental absence. The baby may then incorporate his mother's experience, as reflected in her face, as if it were his own, a type of interaction that leads to a false-self organisation. Consequently the infant suffers a disintegration of his personality (Winnicott, 1967).

In fact, maternal mirroring encompasses a developmental process, which is significantly more than the term suggests. According to Gergely and Watson (1996) and Fonagy et al. (2002), Winnicott's (1967) concept conveys the influence of early relationships on the infant's mind and the child's developing capacity for affect regulation and mentalisation. Drawing on these authors, Clulow (2017) applies their extended theories of mirroring to a clinical approach that uses the mental and physical space between a couple and their therapist, and between the partners. Clulow proposes that the psychotherapist might mirror a couple's experience in an attuned way (contingent mirroring), yet be able to differentiate her perspective from that of the partners (marked mirroring), so that she models a process, offers another (distinct) perspective and creates room for the couple's experience to be thought about, discussed and transformed.

The concept of mirroring seems an apt perspective on the following case, in which a couple could not initially do sensate focus because the woman was ashamed of a genital blemish and wanted to hide it:

> I decided in supervision that maybe they were ready to try sensate focus, so we did, and they couldn't do it. Didn't know why, and it emerged that she had some kind of blemish which had affected the pelvic area. And then it began to dawn on her how much she hated him seeing that part of her body. It was a really unconscious avoidance that sensate focus had brought out. And just for the record, they did eventually have sex and he managed to convince her that he really didn't mind.

It seems that the husband was able to repair environmental failures of the past firstly by identifying with and empathising with his wife's state (contingent mirroring) and then by differentiating his experience from hers ("he managed to convince her that he really didn't mind"), an example of marked mirroring. I propose that implicitly the husband also conveyed tenderness and acceptance in his touch, desiring his wife just as she was. The woman responded by allowing herself during the tactile exercises to see and feel his acceptance and love (mutuality). This warm and caring experience seemed to change her representation of a presumably shaming, rejecting parent, helping her also to modify her own negative body representation. In other words, the partners' creative, emotional intercourse in sensate focus led eventually to their having physical sex:

> Being loved at the beginning means being accepted . . . at the beginning the child has a blueprint for normality which is largely a matter of the shape and functioning of his or her own body.
>
> (Winnicott, 1970, p. 264)

Interestingly, shame is thought to be deeply hidden in the therapeutic dyad (Nathanson, 1987), partly because clients present with unconscious dissociated shame; in such cases, shame, not anxiety, might be the "keystone affect" (Schore, 2012, p. 99). Given Nathanson's claim, it is noteworthy that in my clinical practice I can recall fewer instances of shame in the countertransference compared with, say, anger or anxiety and that poses the question whether we psychotherapists are as attuned to this phenomenon as we might be. Is shame rather than aggression an unconscious affect that incapacitates or challenges some couples in their attempts to negotiate sensate focus?

Below are two case vignettes in which shame was overtly expressed and moderated or mitigated through sensate focus, leaving the couples freer to express their sexual feelings. In the first case, the clients grappled with the shame of having had very different experiences of sex before they met:

> He was very narrow in his sexual experience. And he'd got a wife who was much more sexually aware and sexually experienced, but who actually felt ashamed of that because her husband couldn't engage. She felt that she was, you know, much too sexualised. And as they went along in sensate focus, she was able to express her own sexuality more and she was able, in the sessions, to talk to him about what she wanted to do and they started talking about their fantasies at home. And they really worked through the shame and eventually left with a much richer sexual relationship.

In the second case, the therapist introduced sensate focus to heal a couple's shame about the man's use of pornographic material, splitting off his sexual needs from his relational needs:

> The internet porn was not an addiction, but more about his need for excitement. And his life was pretty humdrum, and so was hers. They had drifted into a sort of miasma of just nothing. I started seeing them about a year ago and we've only now started to touch on sensate focus. But they are very motivated. We've actually spent a lot of time working on the shame, the shame element, and maybe her shame . . . "I didn't do enough. Am I partly responsible for his need of porn?" And sensate focus is helping with that, helping heal their shame.

Encouraging talk about sex

One of the major benefits of sensate focus is that it has the potential to enable couples to talk to each other about their sexual experience, needs, wishes, dislikes and desires. Here a psychotherapist speaks of the sociocultural taboos which inhibited and silenced one young couple, for whom talking about sex was felt to have potentially catastrophic consequences, suggested by her phrase, "nobody dies":

> Sensate focus is about starting a conversation and enabling couples to take in that people do sit around and talk about these things, penises and vaginas, and nobody dies.

This therapist used sensate focus to facilitate discussions about sex and encourage a sense of freedom in partners to speak openly about intimate, bodily experiences:

> It's so permission-giving to be so overt about sensuality, sensate focus and sex, to talk about it so freely. I am thinking about my young couple . . . they blushed the first time I even said the word "sex" and here they are, married four years.

The transition that couples might undergo during the process of the exercises was notable: partners might change from being shy, closed and fearful when speaking about sexual matters to being able to think and talk about their sexuality openly. The excerpt below is a case in point: the experience of sensate focus helped two partners move away from a shared fear of 'being seen' and towards developing the capacity to discuss sex.

> They both wear a lot of black because they don't like being seen . . . and so it's about being seen in sex and about being able to talk about it, and what they found really hard was talking about their sexual experience afterwards. Now they can actually talk about sex and integrate it more into their lives.

Another practitioner described how the intervention helped couples discuss unwelcome and inevitable changes in their sexual relationship. In the first excerpt below, the partners had lost their first passion, implicitly mourning that loss and accepting their new reality:

> Sensate focus certainly worked well with a lesbian couple around the difficulty of accepting that sex wasn't like it was at the beginning, but finding something that did feel pleasurable and intimate, but didn't have that sort of extraordinary intensity that they'd experienced at the start.

When partners feel disengaged or distant, the tactile exercises can help them discuss their disengagement and think about their individual sexuality. As a result of engaging in the homework, couples may begin to talk about their experiences and deepen their understanding of themselves as individuals and as a couple:

> Both men talked a lot about the difficulty of making the transition from their everyday lives into being intimate with each other sensually or then sexually, and that's enabled us to understand quite a lot more about their own individual experience of themselves in the world and of the place of sexual thoughts and sexual feelings for both of them.

Making connection and reconnection possible

Sensate focus has the potential to help couples to connect or reconnect physically and emotionally, and sometimes in a deeper way. A clinician explained below how one couple had become disconnected and mechanical in their lovemaking and then after starting sensate focus, their physical relationship and hence their whole relationship came back to life through their sensations of touch:

> For one couple, a part of their problem was that sex felt very uncomfortable, formulaic, boring, whatever. Now they've just done the first part of sensate focus. And they came back today and we talked about their responses to the exercises. He said, "I think it would keep a lot of people off the NHS [National Health Service] if they did this". And she said, "When I was touching him, I suddenly felt all sorts of loving things for him that I haven't felt for ages". And she was crying and they were holding each other. Now there is a different feeling between them: more united, more connected, more loving, less competitive and less attacking.

Sometimes couples may revive their sexual relationship after years of no sex and no understanding of the possible reasons for their continued abstinence:

> Often those couples we see who have stopped having sex, not because of a dysfunction, not because there's any particular reason that anybody can identify, or maybe in the past, somebody died or a baby was born or whatever, and all that has resolved but they haven't managed to resume sex. I think that the opportunity for these couples to rethink their sexual relationship and to reconnect is something that sensate focus can give very powerfully.

A replenishing outcome of the tactile intervention may be the physical reconnection it can create, helping couples rekindle lost desire, especially if their emotional difficulties have been more or less resolved but their sexual motivation remains a problem:

> Where sensate focus has been very useful in my work has been in couples where there's loss of desire, helping where previously we would have thought that, if we resolve the deep psychological roots, sex will all fall into place. Sensate focus helps a couple reconnect, and it helps re-establish a physical connection where this has been lost.

> I thought sensate focus was useful, I thought it was a way of taking the steam out of the problem, I thought it was very helpful for couples to have a place where they could reconnect physically, if they were able to reconnect at all, and that was the issue. And I still think it can be useful in that way.

Not all couples in therapy *can* reconnect, but if they do have that capacity, sensate focus may help the process. Moreover, introducing the touching exercises might immediately reduce partners' anxieties ("taking the steam out of the problem") about their unsatisfactory sexual relationship. Similarly, the intervention may help couples who become sexually anxious when they decide to have a baby. In such cases, the prospect of becoming parents may change partners' sense of themselves and each other, giving rise to new anxieties that may seep into sex, as they become preoccupied with procreation rather than relaxed recreation, shared enjoyment and closeness (Pacey, 2004; Clulow, 2019). Sex may become more about goals and stressful attempts to conceive during female ovulation. Even as they begin to imagine their future as parents, there is already an unconscious reconfiguration of their dyad taking place (this may also be true of couples who opt for assisted conception). In these cases, sensate focus has the potential to mitigate couples' felt pressure to perform. The therapist's challenge is how to help partners relax, which means avoiding sex for a while, against their sense of urgency and longing to create a family, which may involve lots of sex.

Linking sensuality to sexuality in relationships

Psychotherapists regarded the development of sensuality, defined as the enjoyment of bodily sensations and the search for bodily sensation pleasures (Lichtenberg, 2008), as the essential first step for couples wishing to improve their sexual relationship. Take, for example, the earlier description of the couple who through sensate focus moved away from anxiety-led, genitally focused, mechanical sex towards a broadening out and a whole-body, relaxed, much richer experience. This case vignette was one among many in which the development of partners' sensuality and sensual behaviour lent a new vitality to couples' relationships, reversing their declining interest in sex. Clients' positive responses to this change included:

Touching him I felt all sorts of loving things for him I hadn't felt in ages.

Doing this would keep a lot of people off the NHS.

Furthermore, sensuality had the potential to become part of clients' everyday creativity and intimacy, as a marker of emotional-relational maturity and attachment security. One psychotherapist described a couple who, in times of stress, would revert to the early caressing exercises to reconnect. By implication, when life's difficulties threatened the partners' felt security, this couple used the non-demand physical contact learned in the early exercises to re-establish their relationship as a safe haven, thereby allowing each partner to experience the dyad again as a secure base from which to explore the world (Castellano et al., 2014). Moreover, sensual experience is known to be reinforced by biochemical changes: mutual touching that is tender and sensitive triggers the release of oxytocin, a neuropeptide that calms and soothes and is involved in bonding and reinforcing attachment between mother and baby, between father and baby, and between adult lovers (Carter, 2022; Hiller, 2023). The neurobiology of love and attachment is discussed further in Chapter 3.

It is possible that these psychotherapists' early focus on sensuality was in part due to the modified design of Masters and Johnson's sensate focus programme, in which the first step is partners' learning about their own sense of touch and its meaning. It seems more likely, however, that psychotherapists intended to use the tactile exercises to encourage couples to share loving, sensitive skin-to-skin contact for its powerful potential role in repairing handling failures of the past, and for balancing and nurturing adult partners' innate attachment, caregiving and sexual motivation systems in the present ("sensate focus . . . gives clients a safe, boundaried way to proceed and engage sensually"). This was an important finding because the reparative, protective and arousing roles of sensuality in couples' well-being might be undervalued in the client population and in the profession of psychotherapy generally.

That said, therapists' linking of infantile sensuality with adult attachment and sexuality is well supported in the psychoanalytic literature. For example, Winnicott (1963b, p. 75) clearly focuses on the sensual nature of the mother-infant relationship and their "sensuous co-existence", which makes all psychophysical maturation processes possible, including healthy sexuality. A later example of theoretical links between infant sensuality and adult sexuality is Lichtenberg (2008), who suggests that neonates are prepared pre-birth for shared sensual pleasure by intrauterine finger sucking and other activities. He proposes that human beings of all ages long for physical closeness and are highly desirous of sensual experiences. Holmes (2007, p. 143) also regards the quality of young adults' sexual relationships to be founded on "the childhood capacity for playfulness and mutually pleasurable physical interactions". Once developed, sensuality gives couples an inner resource of security, relaxation (the *being*) and creativity (the *doing*).

Incorporating a triangular perspective

Interpreting clinical vignettes through a Winnicottian lens produces a binary perspective, that is, between mother and baby, on couples' sexual relationships. A quandary about using a Winnicottian perspective in this way is that the mother-baby dyad may be an unfair and implausible comparison with the adult couple, who know about sex, sexual responses, desires and sexual satisfaction or the absence of these. Bearing in mind contemporary psychoanalytic theories of infantile sexuality (Target, 2007; Fonagy, 2008), what might be the differences between the expression of sexual drive in infants and in adults? An infant experiences sensual pleasure, and penile erections occur in the very young (Sullivan, 1926). However, an adult male's erection is imbued with many different meanings; a male infant's erection cannot be so.

Furthermore, a Winnicottian approach to sexual relationships represents a departure from current practice in psychodynamic couple psychotherapy in the UK. Here contemporary couple psychotherapy is largely post-Kleinian and is concerned with interpretations of the Oedipus complex, the third area (Britton, 1989) and three-person, triangular relationships, that is, mother, baby and *father*. Although two-person relationships predominate in psychotherapists' accounts of their clients, the Oedipus complex is clearly and powerfully in evidence in the way practitioners, as emotionally mature observers of their clients' sexual relationships, practise their art.

Acknowledging Winnicott's strengths

Most of the case vignettes in this book highlight clients' struggles to move from a fused couple state of mind to one of psychological separateness, achieving separation-individuation and secondly, a capacity for feeling real, alive and creative in an adult sexual relationship. Winnicott (1971b, p. 2) offers credible theories of the movement from a merged existence characterised by the infant's illusion of omnipotence (a crucial phase preceding the achievement of personalisation), to a transitional third area, which is "an intermediate area of *experiencing*, to which inner reality and external life both contribute". As Morgan (2019, p. 136) explains:

> the Oedipal triangle is reconfigured so that the third point on the triangle is the couple's relationship, a symbolic third, to which the couple can turn to find a place in their minds from which each partner can observe themselves in their relationship.

Moving between their subjective experience and a metaposition that enables them to think 'objectively' about the ways they relate, "the couple can think together about what they are creating and also be creative in thinking together" (Morgan, 2019, p. 136).

Winnicott's (1971b) developmental theories contrast with those of Klein who does not explain how the infant makes the transition or journey from the paranoid-schizoid position to the depressive position. Moreover, Winnicott (1960), a truly psychosomatic theorist, privileges the mother's reliably loving response to and handling of her infant, especially in the earliest phase when the baby is in a state of absolute dependence. He makes maternal caregiving and the body fundamental to the development of mental functioning and to the baby's acquisition of all human capacities (Caldwell, 2005). His understanding of embodied experience and his thoroughly psychosomatic approach to human development confirms his valuing of and respect for the human body. Thus an individual's body, his positive representations of it and his relaxed sense of being alive in his own body, are for Winnicott the foundation of enjoyable sexual intimacy in adulthood. This theoretical stance differs from that of Klein, who places the tensions generated by the infant's ubiquitous and always-active internal phantasies at the centre of psychic life (Klein, 1958). Winnicott's (1960) criticism of Klein's theories is that she overlooks the initial total dependence of the infant on his caregiver. For Winnicott, it is the interpsychic environment which, for example, influences the way the infant copes with his aggression. The parents' toleration of the infant's aggression is key to the infant's ability to grow. This caring, understanding and good enough environment will lead the individual to develop a sense of freedom. The child who is given no boundaries does not feel free, but anxious. His anxiety may be experienced as instability and risk leading to antisocial acts that need to be understood as failures of communication by his environment (Abram, 2007).

Although Winnicott (1964a) acknowledges the Oedipal conflict as a challenging phase in which tremendously intense feelings prevail, resolution of these conflicts is in his view achievable if the infant has experienced reliable, good enough mothering. In developmental terms, Winnicott is mostly concerned with pre-Oedipal rather than Oedipal experience, the baby's maternal provision being all-important, with the father's role minor compared with the mother's. By contrast, for Freud and Klein, the resolution of Oedipal conflicts is a prerequisite of emotional, relational and sexual maturity. Klein (1945) places the emergence of the Oedipal phase in the child's first year, much earlier than Freud, and brings the father, the 'third', into the infant's awareness at a primitive stage. Klein's later work suggests that the working through of anxieties and defences in the paranoid-schizoid and depressive positions is equally central in the human psyche. The depressive position is interrelated with and eventually supercedes the Oedipus complex in Klein's hypotheses of child development.

Modelling the third position

Undoubtedly psychotherapists, able to talk in a relaxed way about sex, model a successful Winnicottian mind-body integration *and* a resolved Oedipus complex. These personal and professional achievements are essential for good psychotherapeutic practice. Couple therapists need to manifest a highly developed sensory or proprioceptive internal awareness, equating to the "psychophysical, non-symbolic, conscious state of being alive in a body" (Milner, 1960, p. 237). Both consciously and unconsciously, therapists model this psychosomatic self-awareness to anxious couples. Their clients need "to achieve an intuitive awareness of an unanxious mother figure contentedly anchored in her own body" (Milner, 1960, p. 239). In other words, couples need to internalise a good object, in order to develop their own self-awareness and relax into a state of unintegration, an early stage of sensate focus, as discussed earlier in this chapter. Psychotherapists' sensory self-awareness implies their capacity to relate to their own self, to be aware of their own thoughts and their experience moment by moment in clinical work. This phenomenon, therapists' subjective experience including countertransference, which is the feelings aroused in them by clients, enables psychotherapists to be alert to intersubjective processes that might reveal couples' inner worlds (Fonagy, 1999). Erotic countertransference, in which a client's sexual attraction to the therapist is acknowledged but not acted upon, is part of the therapeutic process. Couples' patterns for conducting erotic life are encoded in early life. If an individual's need for love has not been satisfied in infancy and childhood, he is bound to approach every new person he meets with libidinal anticipatory ideas (Freud, 1912, cited in Schaverien, 2006). Although eros may seem more prominent in psychosexual therapy, in which sexuality is the currency of the sessions, it is potentially present in all psychotherapeutic relationships and sometimes difficult to detect. Eros is central in the individuation process and may be conveyed to the therapist in myriad ways. Inevitably it illuminates much about the client's ways of being in the world and it calls for sensitive attention. Oedipal love in the transference can be an unconscious defence against overwhelming grief from the past and a protection against being in touch with deep unhappiness. One reason for avoiding the topic of sex in couple psychotherapy might be the therapist's fear that the boundary between being and doing is fragile and porous, suggesting an unresolved Oedipal state. Lengthier exploration of the topic of erotic transference and countertransference is outside the scope of this chapter. However, the interested reader will find informative discussion in Searles (1959), Pope et al. (1993) and Schaverien (2006). In all the case vignettes appearing throughout this book there is evidence of therapists' *thinking about*, not acting on, the couple dynamics and total transference, as they tune in to and use affective experiences during sessions.

Psychotherapists' capacity to reflect potently on their own experience as well as on the experience of others, their clients, is the hallmark of Britton's (1989, p. 88) "third position". The latter arises from the coming together of the parental couple in the mind of the infant and enables the child to observe others in a relationship whilst also being in a relationship with them (Colman, 2007). Britton's concept implies that psychotherapists hold a mental position that takes account of a couple in a relationship that excludes the therapist. As one therapist said:

> You realise that actually the bedroom door's closing now and it's time for them to be in their private world without me.

The therapist's mental stance also takes into account her different relationship with each partner, as this excerpt from a vignette of a heterosexual couple in Chapter 5 shows:

> It allowed her to see the possibility of pleasurable sex. . . . For him, the later exercises were more difficult.

This type of triangular relationship, an Oedipal configuration in the therapy session, provides an enlarged mental space for experience of and reflection on all the transference dynamics operating at the time. It also provides more room for mental manoeuvre on the part of the therapist, since couples usually present with two different, sometimes conflicting perspectives on the relationship they co-create. Although the latter (the couple relationship) is the focus of treatment in couple psychotherapy, the splitting into three possible pairs in therapy sessions is part of the process, and new learning by one partner may be used developmentally by the other (Hewison, 2017), as implied in another vignette earlier in this chapter: ". . . so it was healing for him to know it wasn't about him".

An important additional point is that psychotherapists' accounts *might* be interpreted through a post-Kleinian Oedipal lens, specifically in terms of narcissistic object relating. Ruszczynski (1995) suggests that projective and introjective identification is at the heart of narcissistic object relating in couples who defend against awareness of separateness to avoid feelings of dependence, which generate anxiety.

During therapy, the concepts of the third or third area and the couple state of mind, the complex matrix of a couple relationship, are internalised unconsciously by the couple, as the partners develop their capacity to think and talk about their relationship, working through problems together. The partners can then move away from narcissistic styles of relating in which part-objects and primitive anxieties and defences dominate their internal worlds (Ruszczynski, 1995), gradually moving towards whole-object relating and interacting more frequently as a creative couple. This is elaborated fully by Morgan (2019), who expounds Tavistock Relationships' current model of couple psychotherapy.

Encouraging partners' flexible interdependence

What are the fundamental differences between Kleinian theories of part-object and whole-object relating and a Winnicottian lens? Probably the greatest of these is Winnicott's sensitivity to the baby's total dependence on his mother or mother-substitute, a credible real-life observation, which Winnicott (1971b) claims is missing in the common understanding of narcissistic object relating. This difference raises the question as to whether psychotherapists can usefully apply the concept of the total, unidirectional dependence of the Winnicottian baby on his mother to the adult couple. The answer is probably not; nevertheless, adult partners' over-dependence and its counter position, denial of dependence, are unhealthy in equal measure. It is probably more helpful to think about clients' sexual relationships in terms of partners' *interdependence*, which if acknowledged by the couple is a marker of mature relating and secure couple attachment (Fisher & Crandell, 2001).

Fisher and Crandell (2001) propose that a couple's security of attachment is manifested by the ease and flexibility with which partners move between stances of depending on the other and being depended upon by the other, adapting their roles to meet life's challenges, such as changes in the workplace or childbirth. Their ability to negotiate creatively their joint responses to such changes is part of the couple's reflective functioning, which is a primary goal in couple psychotherapy. It makes sense therefore to think about degrees of *bidirectionality* in couple relationships. Insecure couple attachments are characterised by the absence of bidirectionality, and also by their lack of flexibility, two-way support or mutuality (Fisher & Crandell, 2001). By contrast, reciprocity in caregiving between partners provides a safe haven in times of stress and fosters secure attachment bonds as well as a powerful basis for sexual intimacy (Castellano et al., 2014).

This chapter has summarised how psychotherapists introduce the caressing exercises as a response to the emotional-relational anxieties and defences underlying clients' dysfunctional sexual relationships. Many of these anxieties are unconscious and embodied and may emerge in the intimacy of the homework. By providing a sound working frame and a holding environment based on trust and reliability, therapists may use sensate focus to help work through anxieties and repair shame. Equally, through the homework, therapists help partners learn in private how to be with each other in new pleasurable, sensual-sexual ways, which they evolve and create together using touch and other senses. Pleasurable sensuality has the potential to act as a precursor to sex. Finally when exploring unconscious embodied defences and anxieties mobilised during the homework, therapists are holding in mind both the *infant couple* and the *adult couple* simultaneously. It might be said that in doing so therapists give adult partners a second 'go' at a development process, which, for many clients, has been compromised in infancy. Although adult couples, not infants, carry out the exercises, and although clearly sensate focus cannot truly replicate early-life processes, therapists assert that couples' earliest mental models or representations of past relationships can emerge and be modified through shared tactile experience. As cited earlier in this chapter, one psychotherapist described partners' reconnecting through touch:

> I think that the opportunity for these couples to rethink their sexual relationship and to reconnect is something that sensate focus can give very powerfully.

References

Abram, J. (2007) *The language of Winnicott.* 2nd edn. London: Karnac.

Britton, R. (1989) 'The missing link: parental sexuality in the Oedipus complex', in Steiner, J. (ed.) *The Oedipus complex today.* London: Karnac, pp. 83–102.

Caldwell, L. (2005) 'Introduction', in Caldwell, L. (ed.) *Sex and sexuality. Winnicottian perspectives.* London: Karnac, pp. 1–10.

Carter, S. (2022) 'Oxytocin and love: myths and mysteries', *Oxytocin: The neurobiological mystery of love and attachment.* London: Confer.

Castellano, R., Velotti, P. and Zavattini, G.C. (2014) *What makes us stay together?* London: Karnac.

Clulow, C. (2009) 'The facts of life: An introduction', in Clulow, C. (ed.) *Sex, attachment and couple psychotherapy.* London: Karnac, pp. xxv–xli.

Clulow, C. (2017) 'How was it for you? Attachment, sexuality and mirroring in couple relationships', in Nathans, S. and Schaefer, M. (eds.) *Couples on the couch.* Abingdon: Routledge, pp. 193–212.

Clulow, C. (2019) 'Couples becoming parents', in Balfour, A., Clulow, C. and Thompson, K. (eds.) *Engaging couples. New directions in therapeutic work with families.* Abingdon: Routledge, pp. 34–47.

Colman, W. (2007) 'Symbolic conceptions: The idea of the third', *Journal of Analytical Psychology*, 52(5), pp. 565–583.

Fisher, J. and Crandell, L. (2001) 'Patterns of relating in the couple', in Clulow, C. (ed.) *Adult attachment and couple psychotherapy.* Hove: Brunner-Routledge, pp. 15–27.

Fonagy, P. (1999) 'Memory and therapeutic action', *International Journal of Psychoanalysis*, 80(2), pp. 215–223.

Fonagy, P. (2008) 'A genuinely developmental theory of sexual enjoyment and its implications for psychoanalytic technique', *Journal of the American Psychoanalytic Association*, 56(1), pp. 11–36.

Fonagy, P., Gergely, G., Jurist, E.L. and Target, M. (2002) *Affect regulation, mentalization and the development of the self.* New York: Other Press.

Freud, S. (1912) 'The dynamics of transference', in *Standard edition 12.* London: Hogarth Press, pp. 97–108.

Gergely, G. and Watson, J.S. (1996) 'The social biofeedback theory of parental affect-mirroring: The development of emotional self-awareness and self-control in infancy', *International Journal of Psychoanalysis*, 77(6), pp. 1181–1212.

Gilbert, P. (1998) 'What is shame? Some core issues and controversies', in Gilbert, P. and Andrews, B. (eds.) *Shame: Interpersonal behavior, psychopathology and culture*. New York: Oxford University Press, pp. 3–38.

Hewison, D. (2017) 'Creativity and the couple, after Winnicott', in *Autumn conference 2017: Winnicott and the couple*. London: Tavistock Relationships.

Hiller, J. (2023) *Sex in the brain*. London: Confer Books.

Holmes, J. (2007) 'Sense and sensuality: hedonic intersubjectivity and the erotic imagination', in Diamond, D., Blatt, S.J. and Lichtenberg, J.D. (eds.) *Attachment and sexuality*. London: The Analytic Press, pp. 137–159.

Klein, M. (1945–2004) 'The Oedipus complex in the light of early anxieties', in Britton, R. (ed.) *The Oedipus complex today*. 2nd edn. London: Karnac, pp. 11–82.

Klein, M. (1958–1997) 'On the development of mental functioning', *Envy and gratitude and other works 1946–1963*. London: Vintage, pp. 236–246.

Lichtenberg, J.D. (2008) *Sensuality and sexuality across the divide of shame*. Hove: The Analytic Press.

Milner, M. (1960–1980) 'The concentration of the body', *The suppressed madness of sane men: Forty-four years of exploring psychoanalysis*. London: Tavistock Publications, pp. 234–239.

Mollon, P. (2005) 'The inherent shame of sexuality', *British Journal of Psychotherapy*, 22(2), pp. 167–177.

Morgan, M. (2019) *A couple state of mind. Psychoanalysis of couples and the Tavistock Relationships model*. Abingdon: Routledge.

Nathanson, D.L. (1987) 'A timetable for shame', in Nathanson, D.L. (ed.) *The many faces of shame*. New York: The Guilford Press, pp. 1–63.

Pacey, S. (2004) 'Couples and the first baby: Responding to new parents' sexual and relationship problems', *Sexual and Relationship Therapy*, 19(3), pp. 223–246. https://doi.org/10.1080/14681990410001715391

Pope, K.S., Sonne, J.L. and Holroyd, J. (1993) *Sexual feelings in psychotherapy: Explorations for therapists and therapists-in-training*. Washington: American Psychological Association.

Ruszczynski, S.P. (1995) 'Between narcissistic and more mature object relating: Narcissism and the couple', in Cooper, J. and Maxwell, N. (eds.) *Narcissistic wounds. Clinical perspectives*. London: Whurr, pp. 64–76.

Schaverien, J. (2006) 'Supervising the erotic transference and countertransference', in Schaverien, J. (ed.) *Gender, countertransference and the erotic transference: Perspectives from anaytical psychology and psychoanalysis*. London: Routledge, pp. 56–70.

Schore, A.N. (1998) 'Early shame experiences and infant brain development', in Gilbert, P. and Andrews, B. (eds.) *Shame: Interpersonal behavior, psychopathology and culture*. New York: Oxford University Press, pp. 57–77.

Schore, A.N. (2012) *The science of the art of psychotherapy*. London: W.W. Norton.

Searles, H.F. (1959) 'Oedipal love in the countertransference', *International Journal of Psycho-Analysis*, 40, pp. 180–190.

Stolorow, R.D. and Atwood, G.E. (1991) 'The mind and the body', *Psychoanalytic Dialogues*, 1(2), pp. 181–195. https://doi.org/10.1080/10481889109538892

Sullivan, H.S. (1926) 'Erogenous maturation', *The Psychoanalytic Review*, 13(1), pp. 1–15.

Target, M. (2007) 'Is our sexuality our own? A developmental model of sexuality based on early affect mirroring', *British Journal of Psychotherapy*, 23(4), pp. 517–530.

Winnicott, D.W. (1955a–1965) 'Group influences and the maladjusted child. The school aspect', in *The family and individual development*. London: Routledge, pp. 146–154.

Winnicott, D.W. (1955b) 'Metapsychological and clinical aspects of regression within the psychoanalytical set-up', *International Journal of Psychoanalysis*, 36, pp. 16–26.

Winnicott, D.W. (1958) 'The capacity to be alone', *International Journal of Psychoanalysis*, 39(5), pp. 416–420.

Winnicott, D.W. (1960) 'The theory of the parent-infant relationship', *International Journal of Psychoanalysis*, 41, pp. 585–595.

Winnicott, D.W. (1962–1965) 'Ego integration in child development', in *The maturational processes and the facilitating environment: Studies in the theory of emotional development*. London: The Hogarth Press and the Institute of Psychoanalysis, pp. 56–63.

Winnicott, D.W. (1963a) 'Dependence in infant care, in child care and in the psychoanalytic setting', *International Journal of Psychoanalysis*, 44, pp. 339–344.

Winnicott, D.W. (1963b–1965) 'The development of the capacity for concern', in *The maturational processes and the facilitating environment: Studies in the theory of emotional development*. London: Hogarth Press and The Institute of Psychoanalysis, pp. 73–83.

Winnicott, D.W. (1964a) 'The child and sex', in *The child, the family, and the outside world*. London: Penguin Books, pp. 147–160.

Winnicott, D.W. (1964b) 'Why children play', in *The child, the family, and the outside world*. London: Penguin Books, pp. 143–146.

Winnicott, D.W. (1967–1971) 'Mirror-role of mother and family in child development', in *Playing and reality*. London: Tavistock/Routledge, pp. 111–118.

Winnicott, D.W. (1968) 'Communication between infant and mother, and mother and infant, compared and contrasted', in Joffe, W.G. (ed.) *What is psychoanalysis?* London: Institute of Psychoanalysis, pp. 15–25.

Winnicott, D.W. (1970) 'On the basis for self in body', in Winnicott, C., Shepherd, R. and Davis, M. (eds.) *Psychoanalytic explorations*. Cambridge, MA: Harvard University Press, pp. 261–283.

Winnicott, D.W. (1971a) 'Creativity and its origins', in *Playing and reality*. London: Tavistock/Routledge, pp. 65–85.

Winnicott, D.W. (1971b) 'Transitional objects and transitional phenomena', in *Playing and reality*. London: Tavistock/Routledge, pp. 1–25.

Winnicott, D.W. (1987) *Babies and their mothers*. Menlo Park, CA: Addison-Wesley.

Winnicott, D.W. (1992) 'Notes on play', in Winnicott, C., Shepherd, R. and Davis, M. (eds.) *Psychoanalytic explorations*. Cambridge, MA: Harvard University Press, pp. 59–63.

Wright, K. (1991) *Vision and separation*. Northvale, NJ: Jason Aronson.

Wright, K. (2009) *Mirroring and attunement. Self-realization in psychoanalysis and art*. Hove: Routledge.

Chapter 5

Asserting

Recognising conflict between aggression and sexual desire

Sexual desire and aggression are inextricably linked in the human psyche. Freud regarded sexuality and aggression as innate drives and key organisers of psychological function, and these two instincts continue to preoccupy contemporary psychoanalysts. Consider the connection and interplay of these two drives. A degree of aggression is required in the act of sex, either to erotically enter or to passionately receive another. After bodily merger, partners need aggression to withdraw physically and psychically, thereby preserving separateness and restoring the self. In adult relationships the balance between erotic love and aggression can be precariously fine:

> Where aggression is missing, erotic satisfaction is stunted or impossible. Where aggression is used in the service of love, to get through to someone, to connect by deliberately (and rapturously) breaching the boundaries of personal space and body surface in sex, relationship has the potential to be deepened through mutual satisfying of erotic needs. Where aggression is paramount, eroticism is curtailed and becomes routine; connection between the couple is limited to particular acts and roles, boundaries (emotional and physical) are turned into objects to be used, or used by, and love dies.
>
> (Hewison, 2009, p. 166)

Sexual desire and aggression contain the two emotional states of love and hate. These two states are in tension or in conflict with one another and make the experience of erotic desire inherently disorderly (Clulow & Boerma, 2009). Both love and hate fuel sexual relationships. Love may include the emotionally secure, respectful, caring acceptance of a partner, or the less secure attachment and caregiving styles marked by dependence, neediness or denial of needs, and enmeshed (anxious attachment) and borderline (disorganised attachment) patterns of relating. By contrast, hate involves the aggression needed for self-assertion, anger and the

DOI: 10.4324/9781003328292-5

fear that compels us to seek distance from others. The latter are responses associated with insecure, avoidant-dismissing adult attachment:

> love and hate are activated in different measure by the allure and threat of merger in relation to others, and they can act to inhibit as well as to encourage the expression of sexual feelings. Either state can assume ascendancy, love driving the desire to merge and hate the desire to separate (although, paradoxically, love can facilitate separation and hate can result in merger).
>
> (Clulow & Boerma, 2009, p. 76)

Loss of desire is one of the most common presenting problems in couple therapy. In cases of no or low desire, the fear of being assertive in sex may be a response to the threat of merger and loss of self in sexual intimacy. Couples may have extremely limited capacity for sensual exploration perhaps owing to overwhelming, possibly unconscious anxiety about emotional and physical closeness. These symptoms might be manifestations of aggression acting as a defence against attachment-related anxiety. For example, avoidant-dismissing adults tend to shun physical contact and affection, and other forms of intimacy. Their strategies for deactivating affect are likely to discount threats that might activate the attachment system, and push them to handle stresses alone. This response can result in compulsive self-reliance. In sex, deactivating strategies are characterised by inhibited desire, avoidance of sex, and a tendency to divorce sex from kindness and companionship. Dismissing adults may also be sexually promiscuous, powered by narcissism in the service of elevating their image or standing among their peer group (Mikulincer & Shaver, 2007).

Enabling positive aggression

Where there is significantly more love than hate evident in couples' interaction, sensate focus has the developmental potential to enable the aggression necessary to establish partners' psychological separateness and to be alone without feeling abandoned. This is the more developmental side of aggression that can be facilitated by the therapist. When psychological separateness has been achieved and partners have developed the flexibility to move in and out of dependent and independent states as life demands, then anger can be expressed as a positive assertion of the self rather than an explosion of festering hate and hostility. For some couples, sensate focus can have a place in working between love and hate, but only if love predominates in their relationship. This chapter highlights possible symptoms of unintegrated aggression and the role sensate focus can play in its integration.

Clinical symptoms and scenarios that potentially make the use of sensate focus dubious, unhelpful or harmful may be connected to different manifestations of aggression. In couples where aggression is latent within or between the partners, it may remain an insuperable barrier to mature relating and healthy sexuality. This is especially true for partners who manifest intense hate and no love. These couples may have erected powerful shared defences against sexual merger and for them the tactile intervention is inappropriate or would yield poor outcomes. Most importantly, sensate focus is contraindicated unequivocally in cases of clear aggression where partners are openly hostile or violent.

Promoting psychological separateness

A challenge to many couples in treatment is to learn to relate in ways that acknowledge and respect each other's psychological separateness. When adults 'fall in love', they tend to experience an initial phase of mutual idealisation, fantasy and illusion, when partners perceive mainly their similarities, the good in each other and feel as one, closing their minds to the traits they dislike in the other and to the outside world (Morgan, 2019). Adults in relationships that endure beyond the initial romantic phase may continue to interact as if merged, with one partner attempting to control the other. This infantile, merged state of mind disallows the mental and physical space between the partners who are two separate people with two separate minds and bodies and inevitable differences. When spouses fail to negotiate the gradual transition from their merged state towards the reality of separateness and its inevitable disillusionment, they may manifest powerful defences that fend off that knowledge. Cognitively and consciously some couples may be aware of their differences, but emotionally the experience of the other as separate and different is persecutory. If both partners buy into this difficulty, they become caught up in a "projective gridlock" (Morgan, 2019, p. 103). These couples deny separate psychic existence and feelings of being trapped or imprisoned may stultify the relationship. Psychically the partners collapse into each other, creating a comfortable kind of fusion that eventually feels very controlling and rigid. Such couples, Morgan claims, have a sense of living inside the object, or the object living inside the self, as a way of managing or denying the other's separateness. As a result, the physical merger of sex presents too great a threat to the self. The shared unconscious fear may be one of engulfment and annihilation.

Sensate focus may help couples acknowledge and accept their psychological separateness through play. Winnicottian theory illuminates this clinical process. Observing within his paediatric practice thousands of infant-mother couples, Winnicott (1971c, p. 14) devised his seminal concept, the transitional object, which "represents the infant's transition from a state of being merged with the mother to a state of being in relation to the mother as something outside and separate". Importantly, for Winnicott the infant achieves this necessary transition through play, the adult form of which is psychotherapy.

Couple psychotherapists regard the touching exercises as an extension of therapeutic, adult play. Here I distinguish the latter from sexual play or foreplay in the contemporary popular sense, and also from the classical psychoanalytic concept of sexual play in the form of compulsive masturbation as a defence against excessive anxiety (Winnicott, 1992). Winnicott regards the therapeutic relationship as a highly specialised form of playing, leading to psychological growth and health.

His emphasis on playing in the analyst-patient dyad is a point of difference from Freud's (1905) more asymmetrical view. For Freud the analyst's knowledge filters through her interpretation and illuminates the mental contents and repressed wishes held in the patient's dynamic unconscious, revealed through his dreams and transference. For Winnicott (1968), playing facilitates the patient's creativity, which is manifested in the moment he is surprised by his own discovery. The good enough therapist resists giving an interpretation before the patient is ready to receive it and avoids flaunting cleverness, a move which may evoke in the patient compliance rather than confidence.

There are several ways in which sensate focus may also be viewed as playing in the Winnicottian sense. These are:

- helping the couple to explore and process difficult feelings such as aggression, to overcome anxiety, and to master ideas and impulses that provoke anxiety if not felt to be under control
- helping each partner enrich the self and then the external world through play and fantasy as well as pleasurable experiences
- helping improve the emotional relationship
- linking ideas with bodily function and serving the function of self-revelation, *and*
- giving couples an opportunity to experience separateness without separation.

(Winnicott, 1964)

For Morgan (2019), from the outset of couple work the therapist attempts to give both partners an uninterrupted (at least by the therapist) space to speak about their own views and experience of their presenting problem. If this proves difficult, with one partner feeling threatened by the 'otherness' of the other, then the lack of psychic space in the relationship may be addressed. The therapeutic task here is to help the couple accept that there is room for their differences within the relationship despite the conflict that difference may have caused in the past.

Some psychotherapists use sensate focus to encourage couples to express their differences and separateness in a *physical* way in order to develop a healthier *psychological* separateness:

> The husband's belief was that the only successful sex was intercourse and simultaneous orgasm. Once we'd started the sensate focus programme, they wanted different things, and so I put them on separate levels. He had to experience things that were separate from her experience, and not linked to "well, I'm going to orgasm now, so she's got to orgasm". It enabled them to differentiate far more and enabled him to tolerate being aroused by himself, his own arousal being at a different stage from hers and not having to be united all the time or merged all the time.

In this case, through the homework, the two partners seemed to experience shared sensual pleasure without the pressure of having to have the *same* experience, an unreal expectation, allowing mental and physical differences to be borne by the couple. In relationships where obvious physical and cultural differences have not been talked about, the tactile intervention may help challenge partners' avoidance:

> The couple's communication was poor, and what came up quite quickly with sensate focus was that they couldn't communicate well enough even to do the exercises. And it was to do with their differences. They were very, very different physically, and there was no acknowledgement of their differences of culture, of what they looked like and it couldn't be spoken of. And it was only when I gave them the exercises that we could begin to talk about their differences in a very concrete way, whereas before it had been taboo and difficult. And that impacted on their emotional relationship as well.

In this case, the homework seemed to empower the couple to break their silence about their striking physical, ethnic and cultural differences. When they became conscious of their shared defences warding off reality, the partners felt more able to acknowledge their separateness and the ways they diverged in body, emotion and sociocultural experience.

The whole concept of internal and external space, physical and emotional, in sexual relationships permeates many clients' responses during sensate focus. Introducing this tool into the work seems to facilitate an opening-out and an opening-up in the sensual expressiveness of the partners, expanding their physical interaction and their thinking as a couple. One psychotherapist summarised these phenomena in the following comment:

> Where the sexual relationship has narrowed down because the genital part of it isn't working for whatever reason, it becomes very narrow, very focused, very pressurised, and actually being able to broaden it out and give them some sensuality and enable them to engage in a different way is a really important aspect of sensate focus.

The following vignette offers a specific example of a couple limiting their sensual experience in defensive ways, so that physical and emotional engagement between partners is "narrow" and confined to a small "space"; for example, the "genitals", rather than the whole body. The partners' sexual relationship illustrates the association between bodily tension and defensiveness, impenetrability and smallness ("curling up in a ball") and squeezing oneself to shrink so as not to be seen. In this case, the therapist explained how her use of the touching exercises enabled her client to let go of her automatic clenching of her body as an unconscious defence against painful physical abuse ("being kicked"). The observations made by the therapist demonstrated a clear link between the reparative experience of loving touch and her client's willingness to relax, allowing her contracted body to expand into the space and connecting with her vulnerability in the presence of her partner:

> What transpired was that as a child she had an abusive father, not sexually abusive but physically abusive, who'd come home drunk and he would lash out.

And she remembers literally curling up in a ball on the floor, being kicked. So there was something that had remained with her about bracing herself for something physical and clenching everything to sort of keep it out. So it was almost as though she was repeating that in the sexual intercourse that she was choosing to have. And through sensate focus, in allowing herself to be vulnerable and stretched out, flat, not curled up, she was aware of letting something go. And she didn't understand it. We had to make sense of it when she brought it back. She hadn't made the connection, but then she did. And it was hugely cathartic for her and enabled her to see things in a very different way. It allowed her to see the possibility of pleasurable sex, not quick intercourse, and it changed everything. Interestingly, for him the later sensate focus exercises were more difficult when it became more sexual. I think if you're just talking about sex without the doing of anything, I don't think we would have got to that. I don't think we'd have been able to work with it in the same way. And subsequently they were able to have an entirely different way of being together sexually.

The client's experience of her body was as a source of pain, fear and tension resulting from her father's physical abuse. For Winnicott (1986, p. 5), such abuse equates to gross failures of holding and neglect by both parents, so that the child has "an absence of a sense of living in the body". This adult couple's playing in sensate focus, similar to the interplay of mother and baby, became an area of common ground and a potential space similar to a transitional object, the symbol of trust and union between couple and therapist and between partners (Winnicott, 1971c). The woman then became alive in her body, experiencing the feeling of being real, which Winnicott (1970) linked to the achievement of a psychosomatic life and the true self. Furthermore, the client then became capable of sensual and sexual pleasure, implying the achievement of a key developmental task, the fusion of her own erotic and aggressive impulses and the integration of aggression into her personality (Winnicott, 1950). The therapist did not elaborate on the nature of the man's sexual anxieties. However, she emphasised the couple's emotional-relational and sexual development:

and subsequently they were able to have an entirely different way of being together sexually.

Importantly the therapist perceived sensate focus as having helped create a triangular space for the couple, with the therapist acting as the container of their sexuality. In the first stage the intervention allowed the woman's attachment issues to surface, giving her a space to think about the link between her father's aggression and the necessary aggression in the sexual act. The homework encouraged the woman (client) to play with the experience of her father being both the feared and desired object. Eventually the client rehabilitated her representation of her father, relegating that experience to the past and freeing her to appreciate aggression in her partner (no longer the terrifying father in the transference), as well as appreciate her own aggression intrinsic to desire and sexuality. The result was that she no longer needed to "curl up". The woman's integration of her own aggression and sexual urge illuminated another, unexpected area of vulnerability in the relationship, the man's sexual anxieties. In this way, the therapist seemed to regard her use of sensate focus as having provided a sensual playroom for the couple to explore in security and work through each partner's developmental deficits. Thus the relationship became a safe space for further exploration and development of the couple.

This case vignette highlights the link between sensate focus and emotional-relational development. Furthermore, for the couple, the impact of sensate focus seems to have endured:

> And when things got difficult, what was rather lovely is that they would revert back to the early exercises. They had a special room in the house that they would go to and they'd go back to those early touching exercises that weren't sexual to reconnect with each other. And, you know, that was theirs. It was their thing.

It might be speculated that in this case the therapist was thinking about the partners' emotional maturity, and their ability to reflect and decide to create a space to be together in a relaxed state of unintegration, of *being*. From this position, they could regain their creativity and re-engage with their selves, with each other and with the world (the *doing*). Using the frame of sensate focus, the couple could combine the *being* and *doing* elements co-existing in every human being. According to Hewison (2017), this capacity to use both being and doing to feel alive and engaged with the world is a quality of the creative couple redefined from a Winnicottian perspective. Of particular note, in times of difficulty and stress, this couple returned to the early sensual exercises, as if able to think about their own as well as the other's needs and states of mind and to show concern for each other. This case illustrates how a couple relationship can be containing, therapeutic and creative for the partners.

As couples progress, the physical and mental space required for the touching exercises may be transformed into an adult playroom. For example, in the following vignette, the therapist seemed to perceive the different emotions conveyed in a couple's laughter during a therapy session; he was able to see their shyness and embarrassment alongside their increasing sense of fun as they began to experience sex as play:

> They brought the 'break of the rule' [the ban on sexual intercourse] in, and they laughed and there was a lot of laughter with this couple, a lot of laughter, which is not just an embarrassment and a cover, they are discovering sex as something that they can experience as play.

The speaker's reference to the "break of the rule", as it is known in psychosexual therapy, is the moment when couples 'rebel' in their homework and have sexual intercourse despite having been asked by the psychotherapist not to do so. In this case his perception was that it was a healthy development in his clients' relationship.

Implicitly psychotherapists in my study acknowledged how symbol-generating processes were translated into the mutuality of play during the exercises. Overall, the tactile exercises were seen as a form of playing, which developed a couple's *capacity to play*. Playing is both the process and a developmental achievement of the homework. The case vignettes demonstrate therapists' perceptions that partners' growing capacity to play led eventually to sexual *playfulness*. The latter allows for different meanings and is characteristic of creative living (Colman, 2009); it is the complete opposite of the rigid and mechanistic sexual behaviour that might be part of the presenting problem for some couples coming to therapy.

Enabling the capacity to be alone

In my early years post-qualification, my psychosexual supervisor proposed that I invite clients to be 'constructively selfish' in the first phase of the sensate focus programme. The aim of this essential first step for each partner in the homework was to focus only on his or her own experience, feelings, thoughts and sensations during the exercises. The purpose of this self-focus is to develop self-awareness. Such an instruction runs counter to the expectations and behaviour of many couples who are anxious about pleasing their partners and oblivious to their own arousal. In Winnicott's (1960) terms, this goal, constructive selfishness, concerns learning to recognise the true self, which is the core of the (unique) self. The false self, however, leads to compliance in relationships and unhealthy relating; it is a derivative not of the individual but of the mothering aspect of the infant-mother coupling. It is a clever defence erected to protect the core self (Winnicott, 1955).

A good example of the false-self defensive organisation is in the case vignette described earlier in this chapter, in which the man believed that the only real sex was sexual intercourse with simultaneous orgasm and the woman complied with him, at least superficially. The therapist appeared to be thinking of the couple's shared unconscious defences against psychological separateness, their fear of being alone and their apparent shock of having to face this reality. According to the therapist, the first developmental phase was learning to play alone in the presence of the partner, focusing on their own experience ("they wanted different things") and allowing and managing difficult feelings ("he was furious" and "she was hugely fed up with it"). The homework seemed to create a transitional area, a potential space, in which the couple could allow illusions of omnipotent control and the reality of separateness to co-mingle, enabling the man gradually to relinquish his infantile omnipotence (Tuber, 2008). For each partner, the exercises may have facilitated a move away from a state of ego-relatedness, maintained by a powerful transference relationship between the partners, towards ego integration and relative independence. Apparently in this way they began to discover their true selves, no longer conforming to imagined social sexual norms, possibly a manifestation of their false selves. The therapist described how both partners built a stronger sense of self, which paradoxically facilitated improved relating. Gradually there was mutual acceptance of their different desires, equating to playing together in a relationship (Winnicott, 1971b).

In this case, the therapist seemed to choose the intervention of sensate focus specifically to *disillusion* the couple and moderate their compliance. The narrative illuminates one of the many paradoxes of Winnicott's theories (Clancier & Kalmanovitch, 1987; Abram, 2007): namely that the capacity to relate to and know oneself occurs in a dyadic context. For Winnicott (1958) a strong sense of self is linked to the achievement of the capacity to be alone, which is based on having been alone and able to play in the presence of someone, that is, in a relationship with mother in early life. This case vignette also seemed to exemplify Winnicott's (1971d, p. 89) notion of a developmental achievement, which he describes as "this thing that there is in between relating and use . . . the subject's placing of the object outside the area of the subject's omnipotent control". This amounts to perceiving the partner (object) "as an external phenomenon, not as a projective entity, in fact recognition of it as an entity in its own right" (p. 89). The man (infant), whilst loving his partner (mother) goes about destroying her in his unconscious phantasy. It is this repeated destruction of the object, which is not motivated by anger, that the object (partner) becomes recognised as having a life of her own (Winnicott, 1971d).

Respecting couples' ambivalence

Sometimes introducing sensate focus may achieve little more than bringing into the awareness of therapist and clients alike the limitations or futility of the intervention. That is not necessarily a bad outcome; on the contrary for certain couples it may be a realistic if disappointing outcome, insofar as the partners have discovered that they do not want what they say they want: sex with each other. Therapist and clients alike may conclude that the couple have gone as far into the emotional-relational exploration as they wish, and the touching exercises are inappropriate. In the excerpt below, the therapist described couples who chose to end treatment when they understood more about the dynamics underpinning their presenting problem and importantly were more able to talk about it:

> Sometimes we get to a point where sensate focus is not needed or not indicated, because they're either happy with what they're doing and they've understood why he has erectile dysfunction. Sometimes that means the erectile dysfunction is better, sometimes it means it's no better but they don't mind about it, and the relationship is better, and they're feeling less destructive in it.

In some cases, the presenting sexual problem may remain as a kind of homeostasis, which the partners prefer to the possible risks of pursuing emotional-relational change. The latter would require working through the aggressive feelings, against which the couple maintain robust defences. If the latter are dismantled, spouses may be left with threatening or overwhelming anxieties. In these scenarios, the therapist's responsibility is to accept and respect no-change decisions in couples.

Indeed, the therapeutic process of bringing unconscious motivations into conscious awareness and enabling partners to live with their psychopathology in the widest sense, as described by Freud (1901), is a good outcome. Accepting 'no change' may be the change.

In cases where sensate focus has been introduced into the therapy and not 'worked' for couples, the exercises may have connected partners with difficult or unbearable feelings. The therapist quoted below spoke of a couple who seemed to have managed their fear of destructiveness by having no sex with each other and tolerating the man taking his sexual urges out of his marriage and going to a prostitute. The partners kept their relational distance, which was implied in the words, "we kept working with sensate focus", suggesting that they retained the status quo and also suggesting that they repeated the exercises in a mechanical, dissociated way. The phrase, "we never got anywhere with it" may imply that the couple did not wholly engage in the tactile experience:

> I saw a couple [years ago] . . . and we kept working with sensate focus for weeks and months and we never got anywhere with it. So she didn't want to make love and he did and in the end actually he went to a prostitute and she found out but they carried on living together with no sex.

The inability of this couple to be both emotionally and sexually close is a common presentation in couple therapy. The phrase "she found out" implies that the man's going to a prostitute was an aggressive act of deceit on his part, and not an accepted solution agreed in advance between the partners. With some couples there is also the real possibility that partners manage their aggression by combining forces to defeat the therapy rather than each other. Alternatively, the therapist might be defended against as the aggressive one.

Probably all psychotherapists can recall no-sex couples who could not use sensate focus to help them regain a sensual or sexual connection or become closer. Indeed, the introduction of the touching exercises may persuade partners to keep their distance or possibly to separate:

> There are couples who are ready to talk about it, and then there are the couples with whom I may have made the call too early, or maybe they just aren't interested. But the introduction of sensate focus has brought them face to face with the reality of what's going on, and the outcome of sensate focus is sometimes that people decide *not* to have sex.
>
> Often it's when the couple are at the point of "We just can't do this. Yes, we can get on well at one level, but not this". And for me that's sad, not because I think that they should stay together, but because it's usually brought them in touch with the grey surface of the fact that they can't. . .. Mostly it's that they presented too late. The emotional scarring is too great and they just can't go back and they can't go forward. I don't think it's true that trust can always be rebuilt.

For this therapist, unhappy couples might be beyond help, if damaged by many years of emotional scarring, which becomes a powerful barrier to change. Some spouses feel 'stuck'; fear has replaced trust and change feels impossible. The presenting couple's shared unconscious defences may be categorised as projective gridlock, as referenced earlier in this chapter.

Assessing the potential for change

Couples in unhappy, long-term relationships are unlikely to benefit from sensate focus, owing to the years of resentment they have probably accumulated. It can be too hard for some older couples either to change their relationship or to end it. Might sensate focus be in general more helpful to younger couples? As one therapist suggested:

> A couple with whom I might do sensate focus are a young couple who have been together about five or six years. They've got more energy, they've got more fight, they've got more spirit, they've got more time ahead of them, and I think that makes a difference. It would be painful to break up, but they've got that opportunity much more, I think. They haven't got the years of resentment, the years of pain and the years of not being heard or seen.

Whether younger and older couples can derive benefit from sensate focus is a moot point. Early in my clinical training a couple in their 20s presented with the man's early ejaculation disorder. The history-taking assessment lasted only minutes, providing an absolute minimum of information: the partners' dates of birth and their description of all four parents as "nice and quiet". Unsure how to proceed at first, particularly as I had no idea how well they spoke English, I decided to collaborate with their unspoken wish to be told how to fix it, to have a prescription they could take away. My decision to proceed was influenced largely by their behaviour, body language and attitude, which spoke volumes. On arrival in the rather spartan clinical setting, their first step was to take care of themselves by moving two plastic chairs close together, so that they were in body contact sitting side by side supporting each other throughout the session. They held hands, exchanged smiles, then turned to me still smiling with an air of expectancy. From the start they seemed respectful of me as a potential source of help and appeared to listen in a focused way. Sessions lasted under 20 minutes. The few words they did speak each week were to confirm that they had done every task as proposed and it had gone well. Weeks later they completed the programme and seemed pleased and happy at our final meeting.

As a trainee therapist, working with this couple was for me a pleasant but puzzling experience. Of particular note my supervisor, who was psychodynamic in orientation, suggested that I make this case the topic of my next essay because they were "a real couple and a super psychosexual case". However, I did not agree. In my view, I did not have enough material to write about them at that time. I still have many questions about these young partners: they were my only case of a couple in love who apparently resolved their sexual problem despite saying little to their therapist. This seemed too good to be true. Thirty years on, would I find new ways into their unspoken experience and their unconscious anxieties? I have not seen another couple like them. It may be that a young couple are particularly vulnerable to placing a premium on being a unit, fearing that differentiation might damage their relationship and positioning the therapist as a potential "marriage wrecker" (Clulow, 1984, p. 378). Their presenting sexual symptom might have been a protective device against any upsurge of excitement or arousal, associated with repressed systems from both his and her internalised (nice and quiet) family, which they experienced as threatening to their relationship. As Clulow (pp. 377–378) proposes:

> The marriage can, in psychodynamic terms, be understood as an unconscious agreement to maintain a shared defence against expressions of need and frustration because of a shared phantasy . . . that relationships would not withstand such emotional loads. The physical imperatives of sex challenged the defensive system and so constituted a problem in those terms.

A good outcome in their minds might have been the proverbial 'flight into health', something intended to keep everyone happy, or at least nice and quiet. In this case the question for the therapist is whether to accept the defence or address the anxiety. Either way, sensate focus would not be an appropriate intervention for such a fused couple, for whom the sexual problem "may serve an ambivalent purpose, establishing proximity to hope and distance from fear" (p. 380).

In complete contrast to the young partners, an older couple presented soon after I had qualified, stating that they only wanted to be given homework and they did not wish to discuss their relationship in any way. Unlike the first couple who were alive and engaging, this older couple were sombre in mood, possibly in despair, seemingly wanting to have sex in the belief that it would bring them to life and lift their unhappiness. This time my collaboration or collusion with their defences certainly did not work: after a few sessions they ended the therapy, stating that they had had sexual intercourse and it was all fine now. I had many doubts and felt paid off. Nothing in their presentation during the final session suggested that all was "fine". It was a sobering lesson. This older (but not aged) couple seemed sad rather than hostile, but might they have had similar difficulties with unintegrated aggression as other more obviously angry couples? Maybe the issue for them was a sense of mortality with the passing of time, or regret at opportunities lost between them. Might their seeking sex therapy have been a defence against mourning?

Be that as it may, my own clinical experience is that for some long-term spouses, even those in their 70s and 80s, regaining at least a degree of sensual contact through the programme's early stages may make a positive difference to their felt security and well-being. Older people may be grappling with all kinds of life events, health concerns and degenerative diseases, combined with a sense of loss of sexual attractiveness in old age. These factors are in themselves a dampener to sexual urges and sexual satisfaction. The partners may be depressed or angry about their losses, particularly if they have enjoyed an active sexual relationship in the past. Sometimes the tactile intervention may restore closeness and couples may then be able to mourn their sexual pleasures of the past and accept physical losses, concluding that they cannot go further, but feel glad and relieved to have some kind of a sex life again. I distinguish between the latter and other long-term couples whose manifestations of primitive aggression in couple functioning may never have been addressed and their shared hostility dominates their presentation. It is highly unlikely that sensate focus could help such couples develop their intimate lives and sexual relationships, whereas with some older couples the intervention may reinstate a degree of sensual intimacy, if they are able to grieve and accept their losses.

Protecting against harm

Sensate focus is contraindicated when working with abusive couples who demonstrate unacceptably high aggression in their relationship. The two therapists below described their concerns firstly, about not being able to trust the partners in an abusive relationship to respect each other's boundaries, physical and emotional ("misuse their access to the other's vulnerability"); secondly, about one partner bullying the other to comply with the prescribed homework and not being capable of being kind to each other:

> I think when there are high levels of aggression within a relationship I would definitely not use sensate focus. Also when it feels as though there's a risk that one partner might misuse their access to the other's vulnerability, or where I'm not confident that one of the partners is not somehow allowing themselves to be coerced into something that they're not ready for.

> Sensate focus is definitely contraindicated in couples who are very conflicted, very definitely. I wouldn't even go near that. I think the therapist has to feel very confident that the couples will be kind to each other, that there's respect and trust. While there's still major tensional conflict, it's unlikely sensate focus would work and I wouldn't even try it.

Contraindications for sensate focus include couples where one partner is clearly afraid of the other:

> One couple were really in trouble. He was a very powerful man, and she was quite frightened of him emotionally, and she deferred to him a lot although she was high up in her own profession. And what was really interesting was that they came saying, "We're not having sex, but we realise that there's other stuff to do first". I worked with them for two years. And I never felt with this couple that it was the right thing to do, to begin to talk about the sexual dynamic between them. And I don't know whether I was just being kept away, I think I was. The idea of introducing sensate focus with this couple was a complete no-no in my mind. It would have been like trying to put a plaster on an aortic bleed.

In the context of high levels of aggression in couples, the use of imagery in this quotation is remarkable: "aortic bleed" hints at covert or overt violence in the couple and a lack of respect between the partners, just as the "plaster on the aortic bleed" conveyed the therapist's sense of hopelessness and futility of offering tactile exercises in this case. The distancing of the couple from each other and from the therapist was reflected in her words "I was just being kept away", emphasising how the exploration of sensuality would be too threatening to clients in such a relationship. In her countertransference the therapist sensed the couple's rage and terror. Maybe these responses together with her experience of being kept out maintained the inhibition of any discussion of sex within the therapy.

In couples manifesting primitive aggression, a history of childhood abuse may be apparent. The introduction of tactile exercises where one or both partners has suffered sexual, emotional or physical abuse needs particularly careful consideration and due caution. On this note I had expected that my study would provide a clear stance on this clinical concern. Instead, it broadened the range of possibilities. One therapist described how a client who had been abused in childhood could not accept a touching exercise offered by her:

> He was sexually abused as a child. And a few years into couple counselling I started them on sensate focus, and he was utterly unable to engage with the process. He couldn't be told what to do and couldn't *not* be in control of his own agenda. So I think it was a response to his abuse in terms of not wanting someone else to control him sexually.

A general guideline is that introducing sensate focus is contraindicated if there is significant abuse in the history of one or both partners, particularly if that abuse is unresolved. In the case of couples for whom abuse is unprocessed and aggression is not integrated in their psyches, sensate focus is inappropriate. Experienced therapists are aware of this and are wary of evoking traumatic experiences in the partners. Nonetheless, if memories of abuse surface during treatment and the couple have started the homework, or at least discussed it with their therapist, the traumatic memory might be able to be talked about, allowing *both* partners to become aware of the roots of a difficult emotional response in one partner that neither had understood up to that point:

> Where there's *unprocessed* sexual abuse, sensate focus may be impossible. I'm thinking of a client who actually hadn't disclosed anything and then in sensate focus, when the breasts and genitals were included, she became very distressed and it transpired that a neighbour had grabbed at her breasts when she was a teenager. Her husband knew there was an issue about her breasts and didn't know why.

Such avoidance of repressed trauma in clients extends to the self-destructive aspects of substance abuse, where dependency on mind-altering chemicals may turn the exercises into a "minefield" for some gay couples who have "chem sex":

The issues of intimacy and sensate focus are a minefield for a lot of gay couples, particularly if they're into chem sex, because of the effect of the chemical on them. Then sensate focus is about intimacy and touch, care, and some gay men find it difficult, because the moment they touch opens up a huge vulnerability. Not in all cases, of course, but in some, and I think that's terrifying for them.

Other types of trauma that contraindicate the sensual exercises include early loss of the mother or main caregiver. Below the therapist describes her sensitive response to one client who had suffered the loss of his mother in infancy:

In cases of men where the mother has died when they were babies and as a result they have not had that early physical contact with the mother, then sensate focus might be quite overwhelming, invasive, frightening. In one couple I've seen, it would have created, I think, panic attacks, and in another possibly mental breakdown. Even just talking . . . the husband had a code. He would say to me, "I'm going funny, I feel funny," which was him beginning to dissociate. I think if I'd tried sensate focus, it would have been very damaging. So it's another reason why I think we need to respect sensate focus as a very powerful tool, not just something that we dish out.

It might be that in such cases, aggression that was communicated through the therapist's fear of doing harm ("it would have been very damaging") was also an unconscious communication of the husband's aggression. The latter in this case might have been his defence against overwhelming, intense feelings of loss and fear associated with his mother's death.

Using the therapist's subjective experience

Psychotherapists' subjective experience, including their countertransference, can be a way of accessing their clients' self-defeating patterns of relating and aggression. Perhaps all therapists have had the experience of feeling "pushed" by couples to give them something to do to resolve their sexual problems. In one instance, the therapist reflected that occasionally she had been drawn into colluding with her clients' unconscious aggression, ensuring that no relational change was possible:

Sensate focus has always been a mistake if I've felt bounced into it, pushed into it. I think it gets used with some couples to ensure that there isn't any change, that what's been set up is the impossibility of change and I can get drawn into colluding with that somehow. Then it becomes my fault because I didn't deliver what would have made change possible.

This is another example of a couple unconsciously projecting their aggression into the therapist so that the therapeutic goals are defeated and the therapist made to be at fault.

In a similar vein the therapist quoted below concluded that the introduction of sensate focus may have been linked to her own defensiveness and conscious and unconscious aggression. Her experience might also be understood as her own transference to the couple, as well as her countertransference to the projection of the couple's aggression into her and defence against helplessness:

> I have used sensate focus as a defensive process in me because I'm feeling help-less and I want to kick it back to them and tell them to get on and do something. So I think it can be quite aggressive on the part of the therapist.
>
> Sometimes, yes, sensate focus does do what I intend it to do, which is to illustrate in the introduction of it, say, that the physicality of the thing is too much and so we stay where we are. This is usually when I'm feeling pushed to do something by the couple.
>
> Of course what I should be able to do is interpret why they're pushing me, and sometimes I can't do that. Sometimes I just go, "OK, so if we were to do this, then we could do this," and they go, "Err". So, yes, that might be an intentional, kind of, "Look, I've thought about this," so it might be me trying to gain control and grab hold of the session, I don't know.

Reflection on self and self-awareness play critical roles in therapists' decisions to use the tactile exercises. This therapist was particularly thoughtful and secure in her role, in that she questioned aspects of her responses to couples who "pushed" her to "do something" and acknowledged her own underlying aggressive feelings in phrases such as "grabbing hold of the session". The psychotherapists quoted in this chapter conveyed a wariness of the power of the tactile intervention to do harm as well as good, thereby associating it implicitly with aggressive impulses in the therapeutic relationship. The following case vignette highlights the difficulty for the couple psychotherapist of choosing the appropriate treatment for some spouses: couple therapy with or without sensate focus, or individual therapy?

> My feeling was that both of them needed individual therapy, because they had issues from early childhood of maybe anger towards women, men. When they met their relationship made things worse, because they were bringing their long-ing for some change to each other. I got to the stage where I felt that sensate focus was not helping. It was damaging the couple, trying to force them to inti-macy when they hadn't come to terms with themselves.

Interestingly, psychotherapists' use of language in these vignettes, for example "minefield", "grabbing" and "damaging", repeatedly evoked images of destruction, injury, death and the powerful force of primitive aggression. It might also be that they were reflecting couples' innate fear of their destructiveness, communicated unconsciously to the therapist and acknowledged as the therapist's subjective experience, or countertransference. In summary, sensate focus is contraindicated with couples who are consciously or unconsciously destructive and attacking in their patterns of relating with each other ("the emotional scarring is too great").

Reflecting on aggression in couples

Winnicottian theories are helpful when considering clients' aggression. For Winnicott (1971a), health and creativity (including sex) in adulthood depend on the fusion of erotic and destructive drives in infancy. This fusion comes with the baby's ruthless urge to bite from the age of about five months and is made possible only by an environmental provision that meets the child's dependence needs. A remarkable, almost startling claim made by Winnicott is that this provision includes the mother's reciprocal desire for her breast to be attacked by her baby – in this instance Winnicott's notion of desire might be more accurately the mother's boundaried acceptance, when she capitulates out of love and accepts the infant's aggressive acts up to a point, taking care not to retaliate, so that she might detoxify his hostility. The latter is a good enough environment, in which aggression becomes integrated into the individual personality and fuels spontaneity, work and play (Abram, 2007). However, in an environment of deprivation, which might be the mother's under- or over-acceptance of the baby's hostile feelings, aggression can turn into enactments of violence and destruction, which Winnicott (1956, p. 306) names the "anti-social tendency". The task of fusion, he claims, is a severe one, and large quantities of *unfused* aggression in clients may complicate the psychopathology of the analysand and the therapeutic process.

The tactile exercises are an inappropriate intervention for couples in abusive or violent relationships in which unfused aggression, fear and intimidation are manifested ("I wouldn't even try it"). Moreover, the homework might still be contraindicated in less extreme cases of unfused aggression. For example, a therapist might infer that in infancy couples who had "years of resentment . . . from not being heard or seen" have experienced repeated failures by their mother to make real or recognise the spontaneous gestures of her baby, leaving the infant feeling unrecognised by her. In adult couplings, the "years of resentment" or repressed anger might then be the outcome of partners' repeated but futile attempts to be recognised and create something new in the relationship (Hewison, 2017), with their efforts seeming to fall repeatedly on stony ground.

In couple work, therapists may perceive that one partner's anger, even without violence, can generate anxiety and fear in the other partner and kill off sexual desire. Grier (2009) suggests that if partners claiming to love each other present with the problem of a shared difficulty with anger, it may be that they cannot bear to know about their own hatred. The author proposes that in such cases one partner may project his hatred into the other who in turn evokes hatred in the first. Denial of ambivalence and hatred can lead to a cold, punishing, impersonal quality in the relationship. Drawing on Kleinian theory, Grier holds that where an individual deeply loves his object, his experience of hatred for that same object is too troubling to countenance. Inability to accept that love and hate go hand in hand in intimate relationships and that ambivalence is an aspect of emotional-relational maturity may be a feature of troubled sexual relationships.

When talking about Klein's identification of the baby's "aggressive impulses and destructive fantasy", Winnicott (1971a, p. 70) acknowledges the Freudian and Kleinian concept of ambivalence (the recognition that the objects of love and hate are one and the same) as a healthy emotional state. He proposes that during a key developmental phase, that of moving from object-relating to object use (although moving from "relating" to "use" may sound the wrong way round, it is in fact correct in Winnicottian theory), the infant continuously destroys the object in his unconscious phantasy. His attainment of emotional maturity is dependent on the object's survival of this destruction; survival in this context means that the object (mother, partner or therapist) does not react or disappear or retaliate during this process (Winnicott, 1969). If the mother cannot tolerate aggression, the baby has to split off his destructiveness. For Winnicott, this type of destruction (or destructiveness) becomes pathological. Pathological, acting-out destruction indicates an aggression that has not been integrated into the personality and remains split off, signifying emotional immaturity. By contrast, destruction that is healthy is unconscious and in fantasy, and leads to integration and emotional maturity. For individuals whose destruction remains unintegrated, the very idea of sensate focus would feel deeply threatening, or even terrifying.

Aggression is a major component of Glasser's (1986, p. 9) "core complex", a central structure established in early infancy, which applies to a degree to all sexual relationships. The core complex concerns the conflict in the sexual couple between the desire to merge and be in a "state of oneness", and the severe threat to the integrity of the self that a merger poses, provoking an annihilatory anxiety. A manifestation of the latter may be the client's intense claustrophobia in the consulting room, which is likely to be observed in the transference. Unconsciously, sexual merger risks a permanent loss of self, or the individual's disappearance into the object, as if the person is being drawn into a black hole. For some couples, the prospect of sexual union equates to that of a terrifying fusion, which kills off sexual desire in intimate relationships (Clulow & Boerma, 2009). In these cases, the principal fears are firstly that to be in a relationship means being absorbed and losing control, and secondly, not being in a relationship means isolation.

Enacting sadomasochistic sexual fantasies

Aggression may have a major role in 'kinky' sex, or 'kink', sometimes also referred to as BDSM (bondage, dominance and submission, sadism and masochism). The 'playful' enactment of unintegrated aggression in bondage and sadomasochistic sexual games may challenge couples who want to stay together and the capacity of therapists to help them do so. Clinical experience is that for some, but not all, couples in treatment, acting out aggressive sexual fantasies is experienced as a compelling need by one partner and tolerated with conflicting, mixed feelings of pleasure, pain or humiliation by the other.

The cluster of interrelated feelings, ideas and attitudes that are deemed to be kink are considered by some psychotherapists to be disorders of sexual desire, arising from inner conflicts about physical merger and separation from loved objects (Clulow, 2019). In this paper, which explores links between sexual desire, sexual fantasy and shared unconscious phantasy, Clulow describes a couple of whom the wife could no longer tolerate the husband's ever-increasing need of being tied up, dominated and humiliated by her. The wife's view was that her husband's sexual demands entailed a denial and exclusion of *her* sexuality and desires, and was a reason for the partners to separate. The husband, however, craved his wife's complete acceptance of his sexuality, including acting out his fantasies in violent forms. The dark edge of his desire was that "bondage created a situation of helplessness in the face of an aggressive, sadistic other, who in fantasy subjugated and humiliated him" (p. 9).

In this case study, the partners' insecure attachment patterns, born of negative developmental experiences, and a shared defence system (projective identification), produced a marital fit that bound them into violent ways of relating. Clulow interprets the couple's sexual enactments using Fonagy and Target's (1997) theory on the role of attachment and reflective function in self-organisation. In the case that illuminates Clulow's argument, the husband was in 'pretend' mode, a state of mind associated with dismissing attachment, whereby he made all the rules, incapable of taking another's (his wife's) mind into account. Being mentally alone, he conceived of togetherness in terms of the other partner joining the game as he defined it with no scope for a different perspective. He was reliant on his partner to acquiesce. The wife's state of mind was that of 'psychic equivalence', associated with preoccupied attachment, where psychological separateness is the problem and togetherness conceived of a willingness to enter into relationships in which others define the rules. She projected her own potency unconsciously into her spouse – a desperate defence against separation anxiety and rejection. This case vignette echoes the dilemma of the core complex, described in the previous section. For the man, the core fear was of absorption by his wife and loss of control. For the woman, the fear was the negative consequences of being assertive, that is isolation, so better for her to be absorbed.

This particular, extreme type of coupling risks becoming a 'folie à deux', if partners remain bound in their avoidance of reality. However, in the case study, the wife's achievement of individuation led to her withdrawal from the man's games. In Winnicottian terms, the spouses were incapable of using their sexual games to play with and manage their anxieties. Clulow (2019, p. 12) proposes that "when the narcissistic bond is unable to bear the reality of another mind at work, interpretation of the attachment dynamics contained in the sexual fantasies" is not an effective strategy. Rather he suggests a mentalising approach in the aim of helping the partners move away from a narcissistic form of relating and develop self-knowledge and self-acceptance. Using sensate focus would be inappropriate for such couples, who dread contact and connection with another person and a 'real' relationship.

Other theorists such as Lachmann and Bick illuminate cases in which sensate focus may be inappropriate. In Lachmann's (2016) assessment of the compulsive sexual behaviour of the male lead character, Brandon, in the film *Shame*, the splitting of love (attachment) and lust (sex) is a precondition of having sexual pleasure without mobilising past shame. In such cases, an emotional connection to a sexual partner must be avoided, as with the no-sex couple discussed earlier in this chapter, where the man went to a prostitute. In the case of the client who lost his mother in infancy and felt "funny" in therapy, he is likely to have suffered dissociated trauma and developmental failure at the very beginning of life. Bick (1968, p. 485) asserts that the early mother-baby tactile experience in the Winnicottian unintegration phase is crucial to the infant's health; if all goes well, the mother's handling and holding provide a "first-skin formation". The latter, claims the author, is experienced by the child as an inherent binding force that holds together parts of the *personality* not as yet differentiated from parts of the *body*, as if the body is held together by the skin. The failure to develop a first-skin formation leads to extreme catastrophic anxieties, such as of falling apart or falling into space, which later pervade every change in adult analysis.

Considering issues of gender, sexuality, culture and age

The appropriateness of sensate focus for individuals of different gender, for same-sex couples, particularly male couples, for old versus young couples and for couples of ethnicities other than white European is regularly debated within the profession. In my own training, the intervention was thought to promote gender equality. Since all human beings have a mind and a body with flesh, skin and sensations, it is conceivable that *in principle* sensate focus might be used with couples of all sexual preferences, genders, ages, socioeconomic status, health and cultures. The potential capacity for sensuality and sexuality is universal, although infantile, childhood and adolescent experiences, life events, socioeconomic circumstances, cultural and religious influences and quality and duration of couple relationships may alter that capacity in every individual. Couple psychotherapists can and do modify the intervention to meet the emotional-relational and sexual needs of different clients, a finding relayed by those taking part in my study and which is supported by Linschoten et al. (2016).

Notwithstanding that fact, sensate focus is said to have been created by a woman, Virginia Johnson (Belliveau & Richter, 1970) and is largely used by therapists who are predominantly female. In addition, the author and most couple psychotherapists in the UK are female. For Hiller (2005), gender differences in sexual motivation and sexual urges exist, but there are gender *similarities* in sensual-sexual pleasure; such experience of pleasure is reinforced by the neuropeptide oxytocin, which is associated with close emotional bonds. Her claim supports my own and other therapists' clinical experience, which is that healthy men and women are likely to enjoy the non-demand tactile experience of caressing and being caressed. All in all, no psychotherapeutic intervention is ever appropriate for every couple and it is down to the psychotherapist's open-minded approach and her professional judgement to introduce, modify or omit sensate focus from the work according to her assessment of the couple's relationship and their sociocultural context, as her understanding of each couple develops.

References

Abram, J. (2007) *The language of Winnicott*. 2nd edn. London: Karnac.

Belliveau, F. and Richter, L. (1970) *Understanding "Human sexual inadequacy"*. Boston: Little, Brown and Company.

Bick, E. (1968) 'The experience of the skin in early object relations', *International Journal of Psychoanalysis*, 49, pp. 484–486.

Clancier, A. and Kalmanovitch, J. (1987) *Winnicott and paradox from birth to creation*. London: Tavistock Publications.

Clulow, C. (1984) 'Sexual dysfunction and interpersonal stress: The significance of the presenting complaint in seeking and engaging help', *British Journal of Medical Psychology*, 57, pp. 371–380.

Clulow, C. (2019) 'Sexual fantasy, unconscious phantasy, and the dynamics of attachment', *Couple and Family Psychoanalysis*, 9(1), pp. 1–14.

Clulow, C. and Boerma, M. (2009) 'Dynamics and disorders of sexual desire', in Clulow, C. (ed.) *Sex, attachment and couple psychotherapy*. London: Karnac, pp. 75–101.

Colman, W. (2009) 'What do we mean by "sex"?', in Clulow, C. (ed.) *Sex, attachment and couple psychotherapy*. London: Karnac, pp. 25–44.

Fonagy, P. and Target, M. (1997) 'Attachment and reflective function: Their role in self-organisation', *Development and Psychopathology*, 9, pp. 679–700.

Freud, S. (1901) 'The psychopathology of everyday life', in *Standard edition 6*. London: The Hogarth Press, pp. 1–279.

Freud, S. (1905) 'Fragment of an analysis of a case of hysteria', in *Standard edition 7*. London: The Hogarth Press, pp. 1–122.

Glasser, M. (1986) 'Identification and its vicissitudes as observed in the perversions', *International Journal of Psychoanalysis*, 67(9), pp. 9–17.

Grier, F. (2009) 'Lively and deathly intercourse', in Clulow, C. (ed.) *Sex, attachment and couple psychotherapy*. London: Karnac, pp. 45–61.

Hewison, D. (2009) 'Power *vs* love in sadomasochistic relationships', in Clulow, C. (ed.) *Sex, Attachment and Couple Psychotherapy*. London: Karnac, pp. 165–184.

Hewison, D. (2017) 'Creativity and the couple, after Winnicott', in *Autumn conference 2017: Winnicott and the couple*. London: Tavistock Relationships.

Hiller, J. (2005) 'Gender differences in sexual motivation', *Journal of Men's Health and Gender*, 2(3), pp. 339–345.

Lachmann, F.M. (2016) 'Some reflections on "Shame", the film', *Psychoanalytic Psychology*, 33(2), pp. 371–377.

Linschoten, M., Weiner, L. and Avery-Clark, C. (2016) 'Sensate focus: A critical literature review', *Sexual and Relationship Therapy*, 31(2), pp. 230–246. https://doi.org/10.1080/1 4681994.2015.1127909

Mikulincer, M. and Shaver, P.R. (2007) 'A behavioral systems perspective of the psychodynamics of attachment and sexuality', in Diamond, D., Blatt, S.J. and Lichtenberg, J. (eds.) *Attachment and sexuality*. New York: The Analytic Press, pp. 51–78.

Morgan, M. (2019) *A couple state of mind. Psychoanalysis of couples and the Tavistock Relationships model*. Abingdon: Routledge.

Tuber, S. (2008) *Attachment, play and authenticity*. Lanham, MD: Jason Aronson.

Winnicott, D.W. (1950–1975) 'Aggression in relation to emotional development', in *Through paediatrics to psychoanalysis*. London: The Hogarth Press and the Institute of Psychoanalysis, pp. 204–218.

Winnicott, D.W. (1955) 'Metapsychological and clinical aspects of regression within the psychoanalytical set-up', *International Journal of Psychoanalysis*, 36, pp. 16–26.

Winnicott, D.W. (1956–1958) 'The antisocial tendency', in *Through paediatrics to psychoanalysis*. London: Tavistock, pp. 306–315.

Winnicott, D.W. (1958) 'The capacity to be alone', *International Journal of Psychoanalysis*, 39(5), pp. 416–420.

Winnicott, D.W. (1960–1965) 'Ego distortion in terms of true and false self', in *The maturational processes and the facilitating environment: Studies in the theory of emotional development*. London: The Hogarth Press and the Institute of Psychoanalysis, pp. 140–151.

Winnicott, D.W. (1964) 'Why children play', in *The child, the family, and the outside world*. London: Penguin Books, pp. 143–146.

Winnicott, D.W. (1968) 'Playing: Its theoretical status in the clinical situation', *International Journal of Psychoanalysis*, 49, pp. 591–599.

Winnicott, D.W. (1969) 'The use of an object', *International Journal of Psychoanalysis*, 50, pp. 711–716.

Winnicott, D.W. (1970) 'On the basis for self in body', in Winnicott, C., Shepherd, R. and Davis, M. (eds.) *Psychoanalytic explorations*. Cambridge, MA: Harvard University Press, pp. 261–283.

Winnicott, D.W. (1971a) 'Creativity and its origins', in *Playing and reality*. London: Tavistock/Routledge, pp. 65–85.

Winnicott, D.W. (1971b) 'Playing: A theoretical statement', in *Playing and reality*. London: Tavistock/Routledge, pp. 38–52.

Winnicott, D.W. (1971c) 'Transitional objects and transitional phenomena', in *Playing and reality*. London: Tavistock/Routledge, pp. 1–25.

Winnicott, D.W. (1971d) 'The use of an object and relating through identifications', in *Playing and reality*. London: Tavistock/Routledge, pp. 86–94.

Winnicott, D.W. (1986) *Holding and interpretation: fragment of an analysis*. London: The Hogarth Press and the Institute of Psychoanalysis.

Winnicott, D.W. (1992) 'Notes on play', in Winnicott, C., Shepherd, R. and Davis, M. (eds.) *Psychoanalytic explorations*. Cambridge, MA: Harvard University Press, pp. 59–63.

Chapter 6

Integrating

Challenging the profession of psychotherapy

The previous five chapters of this book suggest that in the 21st century our profession has not formally integrated couple psychotherapy and sex therapy in treatments for adult sexuality and its problems. This situation is at once astonishing, *yet* understandable, though definitely unacceptable from the perspective of our clients. It seems we hold to traditional methods that separate sex from relationships, and bodies from minds. Why have analysts and sex therapists by and large abandoned the conversation that Helen Singer Kaplan began so brilliantly in her 1974 book, *The New Sex Therapy*? Today Kaplan's combined approach – based on Masters and Johnson's cognitive-behavioural tools and Freudian theories, and still widely used in professional trainings – needs updating and expanding to incorporate decades of new theories and discoveries that illuminate the mystery that is sex. The post-Kleinians, the 21st century psychoanalytic theorists and the integrated therapists included in this book are part of an informal group striving to advance psychosexual therapy in its fullest sense by including the physical aspects of sex in couple work, thereby promoting the effectiveness of services. Therapists using tactile interventions need to develop this depth of understanding of clients' widely varying reports of their engagement with the homework, especially when couples' 'blocks' emerge and their experiences are hard to articulate. Could integration in training and practice become the profession's goal? In reality it remains an enormous challenge to engage with professional differences between the various paradigms, and to connect psyche and soma with the personal, familial and cultural spheres to provide effective psychosexual therapy for couples (Clulow, 2009). The profession behaves as if we can separate the spheres of mind, body and relationship and treat them independently. Yet there is a wealth of evidence in attachment research, developmental psychology and neurobiology that all human development, be it cognitive, relational, sexual, social, emotional or biological, is relationship-based and that these spheres cannot be separated (Fonagy & Target, 1997; Fonagy et al., 2002; Gerhardt, 2015).

Is the profession resistant to greater integration? Recent evidence indicates that this is so. Firstly, the entire population of therapists qualified in both couple

DOI: 10.4324/9781003328292-6

psychotherapy and sex therapy is small, as illustrated by the difficulty in locating participants for my study (although qualified colleagues once identified welcomed contributing to the project). Secondly, in 2023 the College of Sexual and Relationship Therapists (COSRT) introduced two separate registers for its members: one for psychosexual and relationship therapists and the other for relationship therapists without psychosexual therapy qualifications. It is unclear how a 'relationship therapist' is required to respond if or when clients unexpectedly raise the topic of sex as work progresses. Although suitably qualified members can be on both registers, the question is whether COSRT's move pushes towards or pulls away from mind-body-relationship connectedness and professional integration in the longer term. From a psychoanalytic perspective we may understand such potential anomalies as evidence of splitting within the profession brought about by exposure to clients who are also splitting in their internal worlds and in relationships. So instead of containing such defensive measures, the profession seems to be replicating them. Might this represent, as Menzies (1960) proposes, the institutionalisation of primitive psychic defence mechanisms to avoid anxiety?

Sexual problems are a common reason for people to seek help. Arguments about sex are distressing for many couples, especially for partners who believe that they *should* have sex or more sex, or should have sex in a particular way, or have children conceived through sex, or have orgasmic sex. These clients may feel that they are missing out and want to be 'normal'. The gap between the fantasy of the sex life they think they *should* have and their actual sexual experience may be baffling, frustrating and a source of recurring relational conflict. So the demand for therapy services to address sexual matters is a call to the profession to integrate its approaches. Three particular challenges face those who wish to respond to the call: recognition, patience and appreciation of difference.

Recognising the dysregulated nature of sex

One of the greatest challenges to the goal of integrating psychosexual therapy is the very nature of sex. There are inescapable, possibly uncomfortable facts that surround sexuality. Irrefutably sex is a thread woven densely into the fabric of human existence and society (Bancroft, 2008). Moreover, sex is inherently dysregulated: romantic love, or the state of being in love, impairs human cognitive capacity, so much so that being in the grip of intense sexual passion has been compared to entering borderline states of mind (Fonagy, 2008). The complex, mysterious phenomenon of sex means that human beings must grapple with the fact that *no one* is ever quite 'fixed' or sexually 'sorted'. This quandary "is part of what makes us human and alive rather than god-like and dead" (Grier, 2009, p. 46). The challenge to the profession is that for many clients the notion of creative living incorporates being able to talk about sex and share sexual enjoyment. Relaxed physical intimacy and affection make a positive difference in relationships and contribute to partners' health and well-being. Sensitive to clients' developmental vulnerabilities and variable need for sexual expression, psychotherapists strive to help distressed couples develop their capacity to live creatively, improving their sexual relationship as one aspect of this where possible and if desired by couples.

Becoming integrated over time

A further challenge to the goal of professional integration is the time needed for therapists to learn how to move with ease between different approaches in clinical sessions. For the psychotherapists who participated in my study, integration had taken many years. The profession's journey towards integrating behavioural and psychoanalytic approaches has taken even longer: 130 years so far. An important constriction is that sex therapy concepts and processes touch parts of the conscious and unconscious sexual relationship that couple psychotherapy, based on talking alone, is unlikely to touch, and vice versa. Each paradigm has strengths that the other discipline lacks. Sex therapy training offers sensate focus and sexual discussion skills, whereas psychoanalysis provides a deep understanding of the complexity of the unconscious relationships within and between partners, and transferential factors that affect relationships in the consulting room. When sex therapy focuses solely on the presenting symptom, erectile disorder for example, this may encourage an approach that locates the problem in an individual to the exclusion of relational dynamics. On the other hand, couple psychotherapy may focus on relationships and avoid or forget about the dimension of sexual functioning. Differences between disciplines can lead to misunderstandings that add to avoidance and mutual criticism, resulting in an alienation and impenetrability that can devalue other approaches.

Overcoming misunderstandings and appreciating differences

How might misunderstandings be overcome, differences respected, and the pool of knowledge and skills be used for the benefit of distressed couples? Firstly, couple psychotherapy could draw on the two major discoveries I made during my psychosexual training; the first was sensate focus; the second the provision of a clear ('clear' in the sense of 'explicit') and containing space for clients to talk about sex.

For all the reasons explored in this book, sensate focus needs to be respected as the enduring cornerstone of couple interventions from the sex therapy canon. These tactile exercises are a *deceptively* powerful tool for some clients: powerful in the sense of connecting individuals with their embodied experience stored in the implicit memory since the beginning of life. In describing his concept 'experiential conglomerate', Winnicott (1968) proposes that the human body is a repository of unconscious affective states. Remarkably the tactile exercises help access this unformulated, preverbal experience. They potentially enable partners to reclaim their sensuality and the pleasure of sensual closeness. I describe this famous intervention as *deceptively* powerful because the step-by-step programme may seem incredibly simple at first sight. Couples' responses, however, are highly complex. Partners taking a first step in mutual caressing may be anxious and their homework experience is rich in meanings and impacts with every exercise undertaken or avoided. Some clients cannot engage in this task; others may attempt the early steps of the programme and stop. All their responses invite clinical exploration. Mutual touching can therefore have a profound effect on a couple's emotional development, their sexual behaviour and shared pleasurable activity, provided that their therapist has enough psychoanalytic understanding to enable her to tune in to and respond creatively to the intersubjective processes mobilised by the bodily treatment. Owing to the dualism that has persisted in the profession, the necessary knowledge of relevant psychoanalytic theory and its clinical application are far from universal.

The second major discovery during my early training was the immediate and unequivocal space that sex therapy creates for clients to talk about sex. The almost palpable relief clients express of being able to talk safely and confidentially about their most private sexual anxieties and experience indicates just how important this is. It is the crucial 'permission-giving' aspect of psychosexual therapy. It resonates with Kahr's (2009, p. 19) concept of a "sexual skin", which involves listening empathically, sensitively and without being excited by or intrusive to the details of sexual behaviour that mobilise clients' anxieties, self-doubts, desires and fantasies. The therapist's skill in enabling couples to talk openly and in comfort about sexual thoughts and feelings, and her knowledge of the sexual body, sexual anatomy and of bodily treatments are major strengths of sex therapy training. The major omission of sex therapy, which has led to its stagnation and which this book is intended to counter, is a lack of theory underpinning its bodily-focused strategies and tools, despite the recent incorporation of mindfulness. Clinical experience indicates that clients are often aware that their sexual difficulties are more to do with emotional-relational conflicts than physiological disturbance, and they seek help to identify and modify repeated, self-defeating dynamics in the aim of improving their relationships.

In contrast with sex therapy, couple psychotherapy in the UK has been developed since the early post-war years within an organisation (TR) dedicated to research, theory, training and practice in treatments for unhappy couple relationships and their impact on children and family life. Fundamental concepts of this model have been captured and updated regularly over the last 80 years as psychoanalytic theories have evolved and advanced. Over the decades this Kleinian model for couple psychotherapy has been refreshed by new thinkers and has dovetailed with the demands and expectations of an ever-changing world and its impact on couples. The core concepts elaborated in Ruszczynski (1993) and in use today, complemented by Morgan (2019), illuminate the developmental deficits of early life relationships, which might become a barrier to making a good object choice in adulthood, and indicate the repairs needed to transform a partnership. These concepts include narcissistic relating, projective identification and the unconscious contract, the paranoid-schizoid and depressive constellations, and transference and countertransference. However, the inclusion of treatments for clients' sexual problems has been erratic for three main reasons: firstly, sex is forgotten about in professional trainings; secondly, psychotherapists avoid talking about sex in clinical work; and thirdly, therapists tend to interpret away from sex, making sex all about unconscious emotion (Colman, 2009). Sex is at risk of being a major omission in couple psychotherapy and *especially the physical side of sex*. After Freud, it seems that sex went out of psychoanalysis with only sporadic re-appearances in the 21st century.

Rethinking sensate focus

In this book a rethinking of sensate focus has been created by applying some of Winnicott's most celebrated concepts about preverbal experience to psychotherapists' clinical stories. These concepts include the state of unintegration, embodiment, transitional space, holding, play, the capacity to be alone and 'mirroring'. Theories of other key psychoanalysts have also been used where appropriate. Rethinking sensate focus in this way offers a theoretical bridge between psychotherapy and sex therapy with the potential to replace the lacunae in each approach and integrate services for adult sexual relationships. This application of psychoanalytic theories assumes that a good enough therapeutic alliance is in place before proposing the tactile intervention to couples. This alliance, or relationship, is based on trust, reliability, safety and protection, and equates to partners' internalisation of a good object. Winnicott names this the holding environment, reflecting his observation that the intimate psychophysical interaction of mother and baby in daily life is recreated in the psychological intimacy and caring between therapist and client in psychoanalysis.

In the first phase of exercises, mutual touching and being naked together mobilise in partners their primitive anxieties about tactile contact, which if not overwhelming can help them to bear their fears, an experience which may have been intolerable before therapy. Couples learn about their vulnerabilities. Occasionally one partner may recall repressed memories during the exercises and both spouses may be retraumatised in minor or major ways by that experience. The homework can then be stopped for a while to allow time to work through the difficult feelings emerging from the process. With a sensitive response from the therapist, clients can bring repressed material into their consciousness, so that it is talked about, understood and integrated. The goal of this first phase is to develop the capacity to relax naked together in a state of simply *being*, a state which Winnicott (1962) names unintegration. He proposes that this *going-on-being*, is an essential platform for the infant's healthy development and a mark of maturity and successful integration of psyche and soma in both infants and adults. In developmental terms, Winnicott is mostly concerned with pre-Oedipal rather than Oedipal experience, his focus being predominantly on the mother-baby unit, a dyad, and the mother's environmental provision for her infant's healthy growth. However, the child's Oedipal task thereafter is to learn to integrate experiences from other caregivers, including his father. From these interactions with a 'third', a caregiver outside the mother-baby dyad, he develops a capacity to manage triangular relationships and be part of a triad without feeling either intrusive or isolated.

Sensate focus can facilitate couples' capacity just to *be*, that is, be present and relaxed together in this state of unintegration without impingements on their going-on-being. In this situation, excessive shame may emerge for one or both partners, illuminating its inhibiting effect on their sexual response. Shame may underpin clients' anxiety about being naked and exposed as having a defective or unacceptable body. Expectations of rejection may ensue. Such negative body representations, which are common, have the potential to be transformed during the caressing by virtue of a 'mirroring' process that takes place firstly between therapist and couple and secondly between partners (Winnicott, 1967). Consider one of the case vignettes in Chapter 4, for example: through the warmth and caring of her husband during mutual touching, a client who hid a blemish near her pelvis changed her representation of a presumably shaming, rejecting parent and modified her own negative body image. In sensate focus, vision and indeed all five senses create potent communications between partners, which if positive, build their capacity for pleasurable sensuality, the precursor to enjoyable sexual play. The whole process of the tactile intervention described in this book equates to 'playing' in a Winnicottian sense and is a complex developmental process through which the infant learns to explore and manage his anxieties. In a similar vein therapists perceive the homework exercises as adult play, insofar as they help couples explore and resolve negative, unconscious, embodied experience.

Using Winnicottian theories

Winnicott's (1960) understanding of embodied experience and his thoroughly psychosomatic approach to human development values and respects the human body. For him, an individual's body, the positive representations of it, and a relaxed sense of being alive in his own body, are the foundation of enjoyable sexual intimacy in adulthood. In sensate focus the first step is for partners to learn to be relaxed in their nakedness and feel safe when vulnerable together. This phase can be the most challenging, partly because anxiety has a complex relationship with sexual response and can either facilitate or inhibit it, and partly because some clients cannot distinguish between anxiety-led and eros-led arousal, the former lacking any pleasure. If this first step of relaxation is achieved, partners can then discuss sex more freely and confidently. More importantly, they deepen their understanding of themselves, of each other and of their relationship, and develop a sense of connection. The Oedipal triangle is then reconfigured: couples can encompass the triangle of their own subjective experience, their partner's perspective and the relationship they create together, moving with ease between these mental positions. Part of the role of couple psychotherapists is to model a successful mind-body integration and an unanxious self-awareness that can resolve Oedipal conflict. These personal and professional achievements are essential for good practice. Psychotherapists' sensory self-awareness implies their capacity to relate to themselves, to be aware of their own thoughts and their experiences moment by moment in their clinical work. This capacity to engage with their own feelings and the feelings aroused in them by clients enables psychotherapists to be alert to intersubjective processes which might reveal couples' inner worlds (Fonagy, 1999).

Integrating aggression and achieving separateness

Aggression in the form of assertiveness is required in the act of sex, either to passionately enter or receive another's body when aroused. Where physical merger in sex is in the service of love and provides mutual satisfaction of erotic needs, then partners' aggressive drives have been successfully integrated in their psyches. In other cases where integration has not been achieved, sensate focus has the potential to help clients recognise and work through their primitive aggression. The latter might be unconsciously or consciously disturbing for one or both partners, who fear becoming assertive enough in sex to engage in sexual behaviour and have a sexual relationship. For example, if one partner complains of loss of desire, which is a common presenting problem, the introduction of the homework as an extension of the therapy encourages lovers to play with their expression of positive aggression. In cases of no or low desire, partners may fear and so avoid being sexually potent so as to minimise an unconscious threat of merger and loss of self. Couples who remain in an infantile merged state need the therapist's help to accept the reality of their psychological separateness and affirm their differences. Sensate focus potentially encourages partners' individuation through playing, becoming a 'transitional object' helping partners to move out of a state of merger and recognise each other as separate individuals. This psychological achievement can promote flexibility between them as they develop a capacity to be alone without feeling abandoned and to move between dependence and independence with greater ease as life events bring change and challenge.

Reflecting on the limitations of the intervention

Sensate focus has its limitations and is no panacea for troubled sexual relationships. Some couples have greater capacity for change than others. Therapists work with and respect partners' ambivalence about changing, possibly using the tactile intervention to clarify their goals. Acknowledging their wishes and the reality of their sex life is in itself a change and can be a creative outcome, even if clients are left feeling disappointed. Some may be relieved.

Contraindications for sensate focus include cases where aggression, conscious or unconscious, is paramount; where it appears that one person is afraid of the other and there is violence; or where there are indications of early trauma such as neglect through maternal loss or unresolved sexual, mental or physical abuse.

Developing integration in training and practice

Despite the absence of theory, some psychotherapists succeed in integrating psychoanalysis and sensate focus when treating clients with sexual problems. What are the ramifications of this for the profession? Professional training is the portal through which all therapists must pass in order to practise. Therefore the starting point for working with mind, body and relationship in couple therapy must be training. In the absence of combined trainings, therapists may take many years of clinical experience to become comfortable and at ease with the two approaches. Senior psychotherapists who are clinical supervisors have observed that, 20–30 years after they first qualified, training approaches have not advanced, insofar as young supervisees and trainees still split sex from clients' emotional-relational dynamics. As one psychotherapist in my study said, sensate focus is often applied without due reflection, and couples' feedback on the homework is not thought about adequately by trainees. Another therapist commented that her supervisees used the intervention "fairly routinely", that they did not "get it", and have "learned in a particular way that that's what they do". The broad picture of professional teaching indicates that integration of sexuality is still an evolving field. Can existing integrated training be expanded and extended and become the gold standard of the future?

Therapists hold strong views about the teaching of sensate focus within the profession and the exclusion of sexuality generally in couple work. As one colleague proposed, adult sexuality, its problems and its treatments, including sensate focus, need to be on all curricula and part of the conversation from the start of professional training. Sex can be talked about from the first day. If this were the case, trainees' comfort with and understanding of the topic would in all likelihood develop into sexual discussion skills earlier in their career. We know that couples who seek help often find broaching sexual problems difficult and are anxious at least initially about disclosing intimate details in the sessions. Their anxiety may be compounded by the inexperienced therapist's own fears. As one supervising therapist put it, talking about sexual experience in detail and finding the appropriate terminology can be shaming, very embarrassing and intrusive for both clients and therapists. Trainees of both approaches need to engage in their personal analysis in order to understand their own defences and anxieties about talking specifically about sex. Given its role in understanding embodiment, in teaching trainees how to enquire about sexual problems, and in encouraging the inclusion of sexual behaviour in couple treatments, sensate focus has the potential to enhance couple psychotherapy. Equally, psychoanalysis can help therapists understand the unconscious processes mobilised by this tactile tool. No single thread or theory is adequate on its own for treating troubled sexual relationships. Couples in treatment require a wider variety of techniques in our professional armoury and a broader psychosexual awareness than are currently on offer.

Conclusion

From reviewing the stories of sensate focus outlined in preceding chapters, four principles for practice permeate the discussion. The first is that body, mind and relationship are all inescapably intertwined; they are not separate entities. A sexual symptom presented in one partner can be an expression of a deeper malaise in the relationship and a manifestation of the couple's shared defences. Therapists working mostly behaviourally need to take the emotional-relational dimension into account. Secondly, sensate focus, if appropriate, helps therapists access the mental life of their clients through tactile experience and deepens their understanding of their inner worlds. Thirdly, the reparative experience of caring touch, smell, taste, sight and sound shared by partners during the homework facilitates positive developmental changes for each partner, changes that can be processed within the couple relationship, thereby strengthening it. Fourthly, the appropriate inclusion of sensate focus and therefore the sensual and sexual body, thereby acknowledging the physical nature of sexual relationships, may provide a holistic, integrated approach in couple psychotherapy.

In conclusion, the impressive fact that sensate focus has endured for decades as the most used sensual-behavioural-psychotherapeutic intervention for couples' sexual problems speaks volumes. It is a powerful developmental intervention that can be helpful sometimes for some couples and, used judiciously, can enhance the effectiveness of couple and psychosexual therapy. Its potential to enrich partners' shared sexual experience is summarised by one therapist who had achieved an integrated approach to psychosexual problems in his practice, and it is the note on which I end:

> I think it's a very useful tool, *very* useful . . . I'm very positive about it. I don't quite know what would replace it. I think it's a way of edging you into a different approach of being together with someone. You can do a lot of work on prejudices, beliefs, fears and hopes, but actually being able to put your hand out and touch another hand takes so much more bravery than just talking about it. And I think sensate focus can really help.

References

Bancroft, J. (2008) *Human sexuality and its problems*. 3rd edn. Edinburgh: Churchill Livingstone.

Clulow, C. (2009) 'The facts of life: An introduction', in Clulow, C. (ed.) *Sex, attachment and couple psychotherapy*. London: Karnac, pp. xxv–xli.

Colman, W. (2009) 'What do we mean by "sex"?', in Clulow, C. (ed.) *Sex, attachment and couple psychotherapy*. London: Karnac, pp. 25–44.

Fonagy, P. (1999) 'Memory and therapeutic action', *International Journal of Psychoanalysis*, 80(2), pp. 215–223.

Fonagy, P. (2008) 'A genuinely developmental theory of sexual enjoyment and its implications for psychoanalytic technique', *Journal of the American Psychoanalytic Association*, 56(1), pp. 11–36.

Fonagy, P., Gergely, G., Jurist, E.L. and Target, M. (2002) *Affect regulation, mentalization and the development of the self*. New York: Other Press.

Fonagy, P. and Target, M. (1997) 'Attachment and reflective function: Their role in self-organisation', *Development and Psychopathology*, 9, pp. 679–700.

Gerhardt, S. (2015) *Why love matters*. 2nd edn. London: Routledge.

Grier, F. (2009) 'Lively and deathly intercourse', in Clulow, C. (ed.) *Sex, attachment and couple psychotherapy*. London: Karnac, pp. 45–61.

Kahr, B. (2009) 'Psychoanalysis and sexpertise', in Clulow, C. (ed.) *Sex, attachment and couple psychotherapy*. London: Karnac, pp. 1–23.

Kaplan, H.S. (1974) *The new sex therapy*. New York: Times Books.

Menzies, I.E.P. (1960) 'A case-study in the functioning of social systems as a defence against anxiety', *Human Relations*, 13, pp. 95–121.

Morgan, M. (2019) *A couple state of mind. Psychoanalysis of couples and the Tavistock Relationships model*. Abingdon: Routledge.

Ruszczynski, S.P. (1993) 'The theory and practice of the Tavistock Institute of Marital Studies', in Ruszczynski, S. (ed.) *Psychotherapy with couples. Theory and practice at the Tavistock Institute of Marital Studies*. London: Karnac, pp. 3–23.

Winnicott, D.W. (1960) 'The theory of the parent-infant relationship', *International Journal of Psychoanalysis*, 41, pp. 585–595.

Winnicott, D.W. (1962–1965) 'Ego integration in child development', in *The maturational processes and the facilitating environment: Studies in the theory of emotional development*. London: The Hogarth Press and the Institute of Psychoanalysis, pp. 56–63.

Winnicott, D.W. (1967–1971) 'Mirror-role of mother and family in child development', in *Playing and reality*. London: Tavistock/Routledge, pp. 111–118.

Winnicott, D.W. (1968) 'Communication between infant and mother, and mother and infant, compared and contrasted', in Joffe, W.G. (ed.) *What is psychoanalysis?* London: Institute of Psychoanalysis, pp. 15–25.

Index

For Product Safety Concerns and Information please contact our EU
representative GPSR@taylorandfrancis.com
Taylor & Francis Verlag GmbH, Kaufingerstraße 24, 80331 München, Germany